THE EMOTIONAL BUSINESS IQ

HOW TO GROW YOUR BUSINESS BY DEVELOPING YOUR EMOTIONAL RESILIENCE

Ally Nathaniel

Copyright @ Ally Nathaniel, 2019

All rights reserved. No part of this book may be reproduced in any form without permission in writing from the author. Reviewers may quote brief passages in reviews.

Published: 2019

ISBN: 9781697077766

Disclaimer: No part of this publication may be reproduced or transmitted in any form or by any means, mechanical or electronic, including photocopying, recording, using any information storage and retrieval system, or transmitting by email without written permission from the author. Neither the author nor the publisher assumes any responsibility for errors, omissions, or contrary interpretations of the subject matter herein. Any perceived slight of any individual or organization is purely unintentional. Brand and product names are trademarks or registered trademarks of their respective owners.

Published by: AN Better Publishing

Dedication

To my husband, my children, my parents and my friends. Thank you for "pushing my buttons" and making me look for answers.

Table of Contents

CHAPTER 1: The EBIQ Method 1

CHAPTER 2: The Solution 13

CHAPTER 3: It Works! 25

CHAPTER 4: Before You Start 37

CHAPTER 5: Listen and Be Heard (Intentional Listening) 49

CHAPTER 6: What to Do When the "Stuff" Hits the Fan 63

CHAPTER 7: Contradictions 75

CHAPTER 8: Rejections and Excuses 87

CHAPTER 9: Decide, Act, Release 101

Chapter 10: Daily Practices 119

Chapter 11: Now Is What Counts 139

Glossary of the EBIQ Method Terms 143

CHAPTER 1: The EBIQ Method

What Is This Book About?

In 2010, four years after I left Israel and immigrated to the US, I had just launched a new business—Playful Kitchen. The business was born out of passion, and I created a unique method for teaching cooking and baking to children while helping parents connect with their young ones. This business was a big deal to me—the beginning of my entrepreneurial journey in the United States, and every client was a big victory. So when the program manager of a well-established daycare wanted to talk to me on the phone I was very excited. I had been dreaming about this phone call for months and did everything in my power to win their attention. They were my ideal client, no doubt, and working with them would surely take my business to the next level.

This phone call should have made me happy and excited, but instead after the initial eagerness sunk in, my emotions shifted to anxiety and fear. I felt as if there was no way I would be able to deliver, and within a few days, they would find out what a huge fraud I was.

Years later, I learned that there's a name for this phenomenon—"Impostor syndrome," and many entrepreneurs suffer from it. In fact, most of them are women. And this syndrome will knock you down if you don't practice the emotional work (EBIQ Method) and release the early foundation the lie is built upon.

Don't worry, I'm going to show you how to do that, but before we proceed, we need to understand a little more about why Impostor Syndrome strikes, and my experiences with it.

Back then, I had no idea what Impostor Syndrome was, or what devastating results it could lead to. All I knew was that in a few days, I would have an interview with this super important client, and that made me want to throw up, and then give up. Yes, that's how bad it was. These feelings made me so uncomfortable that I wanted to go back to my safe place and hide. As long as I stayed hidden, I wouldn't fail and make a fool of myself.

There's one thing I want you to understand—those feelings are not bad. Their job is to keep us safe. To keep us in a place where we won't get hurt or fall hard on our face. Their job is to make sure we make the right decisions; they are there to serve us and watch our back.

They have good intentions, but they are like an overprotective mother who won't let her child climb the ladder because she's afraid they might fall. She won't let her child experience new things because she's afraid they'll fail. She has those good intentions, but at the same time she prevents her child from moving forward, from growing and achieving bigger and better things. Those feelings are our "inner mother" and we need to learn how to manage them, when to listen to them, and when to ignore them.

This book will teach you how to do that.

It might sound easy and intuitive, but when the rubber meets the road things get a little confusing. I'm here to help you understand all the necessary steps on your path to overcoming an emotional rollercoaster in business.

Why Does Imposter Syndrome Exist?

Before we move forward to the how and what, let me take a step back and explain why the emotional rollercoaster happens and why the Emotional Business Intelligent Quotient (EBIQ) Method is the best way to manage it, to avoid time loss and grow your business.

You see, we are born emotional creatures, and there's a reason for that. Emotions have a purpose: to keep us aligned with who we are and to help us release unwanted charge. They are there to protect and guide us to our highest point—our apex of brilliance. Basically, they are our compass.

Emotions are a powerful tool that can make our lives so much better, if only we learn how to use them instead of ignoring or avoiding them.

We ignore them because this is what we were taught to do from a young age. We avoid our emotions at all costs trying to "stay focused" or "stay calm." But doing that has the opposite effect—we hurt ourselves and we block ourselves from moving forward, being as successful as possible, and making an impact.

I want you to think of your emotions as an amazing tool given to you by some higher power—you can call this higher power "God," "Mother Nature," "Infinite Wisdom," or whatever your belief is—it doesn't matter. What matters is that this powerful tool is there to serve us, and it exists within you whether you want it or not.

Take a moment to think about the range of emotions we all have: we can be happy, sad, thrilled, upset, excited, fearful, angry, joyful—you get the point. We have a built-in ability to experience all that without going to school or taking an online course. It comes to us naturally.

What if, instead of trying as hard as you can to avoid crying, or denying sadness, you use it to your advantage? What if there was a way to harness all that energy and use it to leverage and grow your business while improving your life?

What I've learned through many years of practicing different growth methods is that the more we contain our feelings, the harder it is for us to move forward. For example, we might be upset about something that happened in our business—a colleague or a client did something that made us feel incapable, wrong, or blamed for something we didn't do. Our chest burns with anger, our stomach flips, and our head spins, but instead of taking it all out (and I'll show you how to do that healthily later on) we keep it all in, trying to convince ourselves it will go away.

The problem is it takes hours, and sometimes days, until we can get rid of all that charge, and during that time we are less effective and wasting energy that could be used to grow our business. We keep ourselves back by putting too much energy into avoiding our feelings instead of using them to gain energy.

Luckily, there is a solution. It is so simple, yet most people will need to retrain themselves to use the tools they were born with. This is what the EBIQ Method is all about and this is what I will teach you in this book. Stay tuned!

Mistakes We Make as Business Owners, and How to Avoid Them.

What I will tell you now is based on my many years of practice and experience, as well as many self-growth and business-growth methods I've tried. The reason I came up with the EBIQ Method is because although some methods and techniques talk about emotions, most of them do not show you how to release the negative charge to gain positive energy, and only a few talk about it in terms of business growth.

I'm going to explain more about the pitfalls and mistakes business owners make and how to avoid them.

Let's say the past few months were not the best months, income-wise, and you didn't sign up new clients. You're stressed out, upset, and discouraged, and you don't know what to do next. You've tried affirmations and positive thinking and none of it worked. Now you spend most of the day stressing out even more.

You reprimand yourself for not doing enough, you tell yourself horrible things, and you end up feeling even worse. The thing is, none of it works or moves you and your business forward—so what do you do now? How do you stop punishing yourself and embracing the crappy feelings?

I want you to take a deep breath, because what I'm about to share might sound a little woo woo or out there in comparison to what you've heard before.

The number one mistake you're probably making right now is trying as hard as you can to ignore those feelings. You're telling yourself, "Snap out of it," or, "Whining about it won't help." While this is partially true, unless you acknowledge those feelings fully, you're wasting valuable time trying to convince yourself that feeling this way won't help.

The solution is to fully immerse yourself, let yourself feel everything, and use your natural healing mechanism to release the negative charge attached to those feelings. Releasing it is what will make the difference and allow you to get back to work. It might take five minutes, fifteen minutes, or an hour, but after that you will have the whole day to push your business forward. You see, instead of wasting hours, or maybe days, you will be able to go back to work, calmer and focused, much sooner.

I will explain all of this in more detail in the next chapters, but let me give you a glimpse into the natural healing mechanism we all carry inside us from birth: We are all born with the ability to cry when we're sad, laugh when we're happy or scream or tremble when we're afraid. There are more emotional releasing mechanisms, but let's stick with those three for now because they are easy to understand.

To demonstrate that better, I would like you to think about a child who is dear to your heart, someone you care about. Have you noticed that when they get hurt, physically or emotionally, they naturally access their healing mechanism and release the emotion attached to the hurt? They cry for a while and then go back to whatever they did before, looking happy and content as if nothing ever upset them.

How can that be? What's the secret?

The secret is that once you release the hurt you can easily go on with your life, seeing the positive and thinking clearly. The problem is that we are taught from a very young age not to cry or laugh too hard. These forms of emotional release, if you use them for more than two minutes, will be tagged as "abnormal." Since you're smart, you internalized that message and you know that people will not give you attention if you show emotions, and, therefore, it is safer to ignore them.

Let's learn how to regain the ability to use these natural tools and grow your business.

The Difference between the EBIQ Method and Other Methods

My entrepreneurial journey started when I was in my early 30s. I had just had my first child and going back to a 9-to-5 job didn't make sense anymore. Eighteen months earlier, I was laid off from a big high-tech company where I managed a recruiting team of ten employees. I knew in my bones that working in an office, having no flexibility, and not being at home with my child was not the right path for me. While this works for many women, I felt it would make me miserable, and I needed to find my own path.

Since I'm a pastry chef, I started teaching baking classes, and I was also a writer for a parents' magazine. I did everything in my power to build a business that would support us. But oh boy, I had no idea what I was getting myself into. The ups and downs and the need to push myself forward and step out of my comfort zone on a daily basis were way harder than I thought.

Fast forward a few years and another child, and after much consideration, we decided to immigrate to the US. We packed up everything, including our two young boys, and moved to New Jersey, where my husband had landed a job. This life-altering experience started the second half of my entrepreneurial journey, and was what brought me to create the EBIQ Method.

Having your own business can be a very lonely experience. Not only do you have to figure out so many things by yourself, but you experience an emotional rollercoaster on a daily basis. One day you're up high in the sky, signing up a new client, and the next day you're at rock bottom feeling as if you'll never make it happen, while you can't always tell what the real reason for feeling that way might be.

That's why I started looking for answers.

I knew in my heart that, not only did I need to break the isolation, but I needed to find someone to guide me through the business building process. So I started reading books and watching videos on how to manage my emotions so I could skip the wasted hours and down time. I learned about affirmations and Tapping, journaling and self-talk, but something was still missing. I did a lot of mental work, but my emotions were still there, looking for an outlet.

You see, the business world was (and still is) a very masculine environment. Men are trained to do business, while women are trained to take care of the domestic business, which requires a different set of skills. I wish I could say society treats us equally, but I can't. The gender-based messages are still there, even though we're in a much better place than we were only a few decades ago.

I was still looking for the missing piece. I was looking to connect with my emotions, and, since so many methods out there were invented by men, the part I was seeking was not there.

Men are not encouraged to show their feelings. "Big boys don't cry" and "stop crying or I'll give you a reason to cry" are still very common messages, so boys internalize them and learn to ignore their feelings. If you're a man who's reading this book, know that it doesn't have to be that way. What I'm about to show you will help you as much as it helps women. The only advantage women have is an easier access to this part of their being—their emotions, because they are allowed to show emotions such as sadness and affection, while men aren't.

Let me share a few things I've tried that didn't work:

I tried to ignore my feelings, to act as if I didn't feel anything.

I lied to myself, convincing myself that whatever I felt was not real and I was doing very well, when in reality I wasn't.

Whenever I let my emotions out I would beat myself up for "not being strong" and for whining.

I isolated myself, believing that I was the only entrepreneur feeling that way, and that I should be ashamed for not figuring it all out.

You see, I was acting "as expected" while compromising my emotional health. I was ashamed, and I had no safe outlet. That's what prompted me to create a tool and a system to help other entrepreneurs navigate the emotional maze while growing their businesses. This system is what I will share with you over the course of the book, to keep you from making the same mistakes I made.

CHAPTER 2: The Solution

Congratulations, you've made it through the first chapter, which makes you stand out. Why? Because most people buy books and never get past the first few pages, not to mention implement the new information. This means that you take yourself seriously, and as you keep reading you'll take your business to the next level using a simple yet powerful tool. The EBIQ Method.

So how do you deal with the emotional rollercoaster? How do you pull yourself up and keep going when you feel stuck or incapable—what is the secret?

Well, the bad news is that there is no "secret." It is not about forbidden or lost knowledge, and I have no intentions of keeping anything from you. More than that, I do not believe in "secrets" because they do not serve anyone, and their purpose is to hide crucial information.

The good news is that we're all born with a built-in growth mechanism. This growth mechanism is the ability to look at a situation, as scary as it is, and release the emotional charge associated with it. This process allows us to gain clarity, which is exactly what we need in order to conquer the unknown.

It allows us to set up big goals, clean any fear factors, and achieve those goals with relative ease.

In a nut shell, the process (which I will guide you through in detail in the next chapters) includes setting up a goal, identifying the emotions that the goal brings up (fear, sadness, panic, paralysis etc.), and releasing the emotions by using your natural mechanism (getting mad, blaming, crying, yelling, laughing and more), which will lead to rational thinking and allow you to gain a "bird's-eye" view and approach the situation in a fresh way. The fact that you were able to identify the source of the emotional block and release the emotions attached to it will allow you to do so naturally.

But wait a minute. If that were so easy everyone would simply do that, right? And I wouldn't need to teach you and others about the EBIQ. There are a few things that stand in our way: our natural ability to release emotions is oppressed systematically and almost forbidden— therefore, most of us are not using it. That means most of us need to *re-learn* how to use our natural inner wisdom in order to grow our businesses and life.

Let me explain this idea in a little more detail. We all have a belief system that was formed based on messages we got from our parents, our teachers, and society in general. It is also formed from our personal experiences and interactions. Those messages shaped a structure in our brain that I like to call "the glasses."

That means that each one of us interprets reality based on the "glasses" they were handed when they were very young. Why is that a problem? Because we received those glasses before we turned six-years-old, and that means that we judge the world based on a six-year-old's perspective—we let a six-year-old lead, and that's simply irrational and stopping us from achieving greatness.

There's one thing we all have to be clear about—reality is benign. It's neither good nor bad. It just is (unless there's a real life threatening situation, which is rare in the US and other developed countries), but we interpret the events that occur around us and to us through our "glasses" and based on our own experiences and beliefs.

For example: if you were told you are stupid and you'll never be as good as others, or if you were dyslexic and failed your exams, or if you were told girls can't do certain things or they are not as smart or strong as boys, it brought about a belief in that in you. As young children we have no way of knowing what's true or false and we simply believe what adults tell us. So when the opportunity knocks, all you think about (and these are subconscious thoughts) is that this is not right for you because you're incapable: you're not smart enough, or you're the wrong gender, or there's no way for you to succeed because you've failed so many times.

Your "glasses" set your path because they create your perception of reality and that is based on your past. If you learn how to release the feelings attached to the perception, you will see the world differently, and, therefore, try to achieve new things. Things you never thought you could.

How Does It Work?

After giving you so much information and theory it is time to dive into practicality. So how does the EBIQ Method work?

The EBIQ Method has four major steps that I will share now, and will later reveal the plan and system you need to follow to make sure you're using it correctly. As I mentioned earlier, there is a significant part of re-learning involved in the process. This means that you have everything you need inside you, but you need to gain access to it. You need to unveil your inner wisdom in order to gain access to your emotions and to release them efficiently.

So here are the steps:

1. Identify the emotion that's stopping you from moving

forward. (Are you mad, hurt, jealous?)
2. Release the emotion to untangle the block. (Cry, laugh, hit pillows, etc.)
3. Look at the situation through fresh eyes to re-evaluate your next move.
4. Act.

Let me explain each step in more detail:

1. Identify the emotion that's stopping you from moving forward.

Angela, a friend of mine, won a long-awaited job. She had just launched her business a few months back and was reaching out to potential clients ever since. Angela knew she had a unique and fresh method of teaching children and couldn't wait to spread the word among local daycares.

After months of waiting, she finally got a phone call from a local, well-known daycare. They wanted to interview her to see whether she was a good match for their prestigious summer camp program.

Angela was so excited she called me right away to celebrate, and we did. But it wasn't too long before Angela's self-doubt kicked in. After less than a day, she felt this whole thing might have been a big mistake and that she should call them back and come up with an excuse as to why she couldn't do it. You see, as much as Angela wanted the job, winning it was a totally different story.

I knew that all Angela needed was to identify the emotional piece that caused this self-doubt and to release it. After all, she was more than capable and she had a fantastic program. So, I listened to her while she tried to reach inside herself and pinpoint the blocking emotion.

What Angela noticed was that she was scared of being humiliated. In her mind they had already rejected her after the interview, and she couldn't deal with the humiliation, which reminded her of an incident when she was much younger. When Angela was able to tell the current situation was very different from her past experiences, she moved on to the next step.

2. **Release the emotion to untangle the block. (Cry, laugh, hit pillows, etc.)**

This notion of humiliation was so powerful, it took Angela back to when she was a little girl and was humiliated by her teacher for not solving a math problem correctly.

Although the situation was completely different, it had enough similarities to her early experience (school and being "judged" for something she did) and that was why she felt it might be better to quit.

I listened to Angela while she released that fear of being humiliated. She cried for ten or fifteen minutes, while I simply sat next to her, not trying to stop her.

3. Look at the situation through fresh eyes to re-evaluate your next move.

After pinpointing the block and releasing the emotional component, Angela went back to the current situation and realized she was not that little girl anymore and that she was very good at what she did. She knew that even if they didn't hire her, it was not about humiliation, and she could use this experience to grow—she could ask them, for example, "What should I have done differently to win that job?" And then she could implement that to improve her services.

She felt much more confident and less sensitive and that was what allowed her to move to the next step.

4. Act.

Angela called the daycare to schedule an interview. This might sound simplistic or easy to do, but she had been putting it on hold for five whole days because she couldn't bring herself to pick up the phone.

Angela got the job and has won many other opportunities since then. She used the EBIQ Method process to get rid of emotional charge and grow her business.

How Using the EBIQ Method Will Help You Grow Your Business

When I first started practicing EBIQ, I was amazed by how quickly I saw results. It was not another coaching program I purchased that took months to implement. The results were almost immediate and they affected not only my business, but my personal life, as well.

Like in Angela's story, it was a matter of hours or days before I took action and achieved another milestone for my business, rather than wasting hours being paralyzed by something I did not completely understand.

The EBIQ Method allows you to have a big vision, gain clarity, and act. This system is so unique because of the fact that so many business owners get stuck because they cannot bring themselves to *act*.

Here's what you will gain by using the EBIQ Method as part of your daily business practices:
- You will be able to make quick decisions
- You'll cut down wasted time by up to 80%
- You'll have clarity of your vision and how to achieve

your goals
- You'll be able to manage the emotional rollercoaster efficiently and avoid the "entrepreneur paralysis"
- You'll grow your support network and be a part of a sisterhood
- You'll get more returning and new clients
- You'll be able to increase your fees and sell five digit packages

How This Solution Works For Others

After I started using the EBIQ Method and saw great results for myself, I felt confident enough to share the system with a few of my friends and colleagues. I shared the why, what, and how, and I set up a support group where we used that tool to move our businesses forward.

There's one thing I want to be clear about before we progress; there's pre-work that needs to be done before you can use the tool. That includes learning the theory and practicing the tool—I will get to that later. When you join a support group you'll first need to go through a fundamental course, and once you graduate you'll be able to join one of the ongoing mastermind support groups around the country or online.

One of the first people I taught this tool to was my friend Dara. Dara is a super talented coach who helps parents build and maintain great relationships with their children. As great as she is at what she does, she struggles with reaching out to new clients. Every time she needed to pick up the phone she experienced a struggle that threw her off course. Although she knew the only way to get new business was to speak to people, she had a very hard time forcing herself to do so.

As a result, her business didn't grow, she felt stuck and considered going back to corporate, which she hated. She was miserable, unfulfilled, and felt like a failure.

At that point I offered to teach her the EBIQ Method and, since she had nothing to lose, she said "Yes" right away. You see, she loved what she did and she wanted to grow her business, but something was stopping her from growing. All the "do this, do that" advice she got from coaches didn't help because she wasn't able to get herself to actually implement the ideas.

This is exactly why I offered to teach her—she was smart, capable, and a true professional, but there was a missing link.

You see, many coaches teach you the "what" but not "how" to get over the emotional block that stops you from acting on their advice and reaching your goals. That's why so many people who purchase business-coaching programs never achieve the results they want. *Knowing* what to do and *doing* it are two different things and the missing link is the EBIQ.

Dara, who's also a go-getter, decided to follow my lead and use the EBIQ, although it felt strange at the beginning. You see, showing emotions in public (with one other person or a group) is not an easy thing to do—you have to have complete trust and be willing to show vulnerability.

But Dara dove full force into releasing her blocking emotions. Some days she cried, other days she laughed, and once she spent about thirty minutes fantasizing about having millions of dollars so she wouldn't need to pick up the phone ever again! She gained new perspective, looked at herself in a different light, and decided to stick with her business. She grew her income by 30% within the first month of using the tool, and she now has a busy practice in her town—she helps parents create better relationships with their children. Her dream goal achieved.

All that wouldn't have been possible for her without the EBIQ. Now she's using this tool on a regular basis and she's part of my mastermind support-group.

Chapter Summary

1. We interpret reality based on the "glasses" we were handed when we were very young. Those glasses are shaped by our belief system and they create our perception of reality.
2. Perception and emotions are tangled and releasing the emotions will create a new and more realistic view of the situation.
3. The EBIQ Method has four steps: Identify the emotion, Release it, Re-evaluate the situation, and Act on your decision.

CHAPTER 3: It Works!

Now that you know all about the "glasses" and perception, you have a better understanding of your own beliefs and experiences and where they come from. In this chapter I'll talk about why showing or sharing emotions with other people can be hard. Based on my clients' as well as my own experience, I can say that your past experiences have probably taught you that you'll be ridiculed or called names if you shed a tear or show how scared you are. You likely feel that doing that, although it's natural, will label you as "unstable" or "not normal," and you avoid that at all costs as a result. I totally get it. I was in that place for many years before I came up with the EBIQ Method and started my movement to help business owners grow their businesses.

    You might be asking yourself—how can the EBIQ Method help me grow my business? How can being emotional and vulnerable help you take your business to the next level when emotions and business should be separated? This belief, by the way, is a very masculine belief—when you do business you have to put your poker face on and show nothing, otherwise you'll lose the deal. This is what we were all taught for many years, and that's why it's stuck with us. This is the reason you feel skeptical about this idea of using emotions and vulnerability as a tool to grow your business.

Here's an example: Jenny contacted me a few years back because she had an amazing idea for a book, which she wanted to use to launch her mentoring business. She'd had this idea for many years, and she knew the right time had come, so she signed the contract and we started working toward achieving her goal. Jenny wanted to write a book because it would give her credibility and brand her as the go-to-expert, so she put all her enthusiasm into writing. It took her a few days and then it hit her…writer's block.

You're probably nodding your head right now—you know how it feels to get stuck. You know how frustrating this can be. Just wait until I'll tell you how to solve this problem. I'll dive into the solution step-by-step soon, but first let me tell you something about "blocks."

Any type of block you experience in your life, or in your business, is just a fear coming up to the surface, trying to prevent you from taking risks. People have been using this excuse for ages because it is socially acceptable; you're so afraid to finish your book because that means that everybody will know what you think and you will no longer be able to hide it, so you use writers' block as an excuse. Don't get me wrong—it *feels* real, but unless you untangle and release the fear of showing yourself, you will not move forward. This is exactly what happened to Jenny.

Luckily, we were able to identify Jenny's pattern; not showing who she really was made her feel safe, made her feel at home. In her family, she was never praised for speaking up and often scolded for being a "smart ass," so she learned to stay quiet.

Using the EBIQ Method, Jenny was able to release that pattern, move forward, and get her book published. She allowed herself to be mad for two days; she yelled and cursed and cried and that emotional release enabled her to move forward. She realized she could be big and loud and that speaking up was what would take her from where she was to where she wanted to be.

The EBIQ Method is about releasing emotions and that means crying, laughing, yelling, hitting pillows, and other techniques I will detail later. It is about connecting to the core of our being so we can remove blocks, take actions, and grow our businesses.

It's Harder Than You Think

What I've just described sounds simple—all you need to do is let out your emotions and that's it. You release the block and now you're ready to conquer the world. But if it were so simple people would do it naturally, and I wouldn't have a reason to write this book. We'd all be successful in every aspect of our life, but that's not the case, unfortunately.

I know that to some of you this whole concept might sound scary or even crazy, and I get where this comes from. I felt the same way many years back when I was first exposed to the idea of showing emotions in public. Though this was more of a group setting, in truth, I was still putting myself out there.

I felt weird, but at the same time I felt right. My gut feeling was strong, and I tend to trust my gut, so I stuck with the group.

Allow me to take it a little further and explain something so it makes more sense. Showing emotion in front of other people is scary because most of us can't take that for too long. If you cry, good chances are the person next to you will "shush" you and try to stop you from crying. Look at little babies—no one lets them cry. We try to stop the noise because we can't take it, while crying itself is not the hurt but the emotional release.

Let me give you an example: a little girl gets hurt while

playing outside—she fell from the swing and scratched her knee, so she starts crying, and her parent is trying to stop the tears. They're doing that because that's what they were trained to do and that's how their parents and teachers treated them. If they held her, made her feel safe, and let her cry for two, five, or even twenty minutes, she would simply get rid of the hurt and go back to play as if nothing happened. The problem is most parents were not raised that way, and they don't know how to simply be there and listen, so they concentrate on stopping the crying. That's how we learn showing emotion is a bad thing, and we learn to talk ourselves out of that as we grow.

No small wonder that what I'm about to teach you might make you a bit uncomfortable at the start.

This book will offer a different approach to business growth, an alternative to the common methods taught by business mentors. That's not to say that all the other methods are wrong, not at all, but we'll add another layer on top of them, or, rather, teach you the missing link between setting up goals and achieving them—the twilight zone where most people give up on their business because they can't handle the emotional rollercoaster.

This is the exact method I used to get my business to where I am today, and if it weren't for the ability to manage my emotions I would never have become a bestselling author, business mentor, and the creator of the EBIQ Method movement.

I've Been There... A Personal Experience

When I first moved to the US, I was 35-years-old and had two young children. I made the decision to immigrate because I felt that was the right thing to do for the future of my family. This might sound like a nice experience, but I knew little about the hardships I would encounter as an entrepreneur.

This bold move made me into a stay-at-home mom, took away my one most important strength—my language—and put me in a position where my professional background did not matter anymore. I had to start everything from scratch and reinvent myself while not being able to work since our Visa did not allow me to make money in the US. I sure had a lot of time to think.

Not only that, but this type of situation where you're 100% dependent on your spouse, something I was not used to, can put you in a very dark place, especially if you are a visionary, entrepreneur, and feminist.

Not long after, I gave birth to a baby girl, my third child.

But I hated every moment of being a stay-at-home-mom and couldn't wait to get my Green Card, which happened two and a half years later. That's when I started my first US based business—Playful Kitchen.

But starting a business in a foreign country was harder than I expected; I had no connections at all, my English was basic, and I had to market myself to school systems. I knew what I was supposed to do, but fear and self-doubt were present every minute of the day. More than that, I had only five hours a week to make it happen, when my daughter was at daycare. Starting a business with only five hours a week sounds almost impossible, looking back on it now.

The only thing that helped me make it happen, believe in myself, and get over my self-doubt was EBIQ. I had a listening partner (I will tell you more about that partnership in the next chapters) and it allowed me to deal with the ups and downs that scared the hell out of me, so I could not only dream big but also execute my dreams.

It Doesn't Have to Be So Hard

I have a confession to make. For many years I was not very good at asking for help. I tried to do things by myself, and I thought that asking for help was a weakness, especially when it came to building and operating a business.

Most of the business people I knew were men, and the few business women out there acted like men, which didn't feel right to me. I didn't connect with the masculine energy, and I felt small, insignificant, as if there was something wrong with me. But, mostly, I felt I didn't have the necessary skills to build a business, even though I had graduated business school, worked in a high-tech company, and managed teams.

I spent days feeling bad about myself, and for no apparent reason. Now, I know many of those feelings are connected to feminine patterns and to messages we get from the moment we are born, but I'll get to that later.

Learning about the EBIQ method will help you become part of a supportive community with the goal to help women free themselves from inhibiting patterns. Patterns that hold them back from becoming leaders in their businesses and communities. It is about creating a support system of women who speak the same language and understand the importance of managing the emotional rollercoaster in order to succeed in business and life.

Reading this book is the first step of putting yourself first. Once you're done you'll know what to do, and you'll be able to use that tool by yourself, or better yet with another person who understands what you're trying to achieve and is trying to do the same.

The Journey

In this book I share the journey I've been through—how I came to be who I am today, and how I used the EBIQ Method to help as many women as possible do the same.

For many years, I was like everyone else. I internalized the rules and messages such as "crying will not help," "stop crying or I will give you a reason to cry" and "stop being so emotional." The examples I'm giving are mostly about crying, because this is the most common emotion and the easiest to explain, but showing anger, laughing too hard, and even shaking when afraid are also not accepted for more than a few short moments. I learned to hide my feelings and to stop myself from showing them. I even had this little voice in my head telling me not to feel sorry for myself and to "snap out of it" whenever I was down. Raise your hand if you've ever heard that annoying voice.

After the first rush of excitement that lasted a few weeks

following the start of my business, I bumped into the harsh reality of not succeeding at everything I did, not having enough clients, and getting rejected by potential clients and collaborators. These are things that every business owner will experience—it is simply part of the journey, but that doesn't matter in the sense of the feelings it brings up.

Although I knew all those rejections and failures happen to everyone, and every "no" is another step on the way up to get a "yes," it didn't make me feel better. It was perfectly logical, but my heart was heavy and my stomach roiling. Sometimes a "no" could paralyze me for a good hour, or make me feel so bad I had to take a nap. Taking a nap, although a good idea when tired, is wasted time if you use it as an escape. Once I developed the EBIQ Method and used it more and more to grow my business, I needed fewer and fewer naps.

As a result of wasting so much time, my business grew at a slower pace and I felt even worse. This type of vicious circle of feeling bad, wasting time, and feeling even worse was a trap, and I had to find a way to break the cycle and manage the feelings that kept me from growing my business.

Don't get me wrong, I did a *lot*. I created a marketing plan, I wrote promotional materials, I contacted potential clients, I made phone calls, and I went out for networking events. I did all that and more, but stepping out of your comfort zone—and this was stepping out of my comfort zone big time, because I had to do all that in English, which was not my mother tongue, and in a new country where I had no connections—was harsh for me and I had to fight hard to stay focused and move forward.

Some days I felt like staying in bed and ignoring the harsh reality of needing to grow my business. You see, I wasted precious time because I didn't know how to get rid of all the emotions that flooded my brain, stomach, and heart, so I had to wait until they went away, and that could take hours or even days. Trying to ignore them took so much energy I was not able to move forward. I invested my energy in trying *not* to feel bad instead of simply growing my business.

Once I invented EBIQ, started using it, and teaching it to other people, the amount of time I save added almost eight hours to my week. Eight hours! When I was able to focus on my business growth. I simply needed only five to twenty minutes to deal with whatever brought up the feeling that got me stuck. In only a few minutes I saved hours of frustration because I got rid of the mental hurdle that slowed me down. This is something you must learn how to do if you want to be more efficient and grow your business.

Ally Nathaniel

CHAPTER 4: Before You Start

In this chapter, I will take you through the EBIQ Method basics, so we'll be speaking the same language. It is important to me that as many women as possible will be able to use it and make a difference in their lives.

Before I dive into the *how,* I want you to know that there's a big difference between wanting to be an entrepreneur and owning your own business. The difference is the same gap between a fantasy and reality, and it can be overwhelming.

When we start a business it's usually because we want to have more freedom—to wake up a little later, work late, or pick up the kids from school every day. We start a business because we want to do things differently and, even better, make more money while enjoying those benefits.

The reality is most times having your own business is harder than you could have ever imagined. Getting new clients, paying bills, and marketing yourself is brand new territory, and it takes tremendous amounts of emotional energy. The days when you got paid every other week are over, and it is up to you to make sure you bring in enough income to cover basic expenses. Sometimes you'll find yourself struggling to pay the bills, let alone pay for a dream vacation. You're under a lot of pressure, and that's exactly when the rollercoaster from confidence to panic starts.

We all experience those rollercoasters; one day you're up in the sky signing up a new client, and the next day you're at rock bottom wondering why in the world you got yourself into that. You have a big vision, and you want to make a difference and help people, but not having stability and doubting yourself takes its toll. The ups and downs make you doubt whether you have what it takes, and you even consider going back to corporate.

Like I said, we all experience those feelings, but some of us keep going, building successful businesses while others quit. So what's the secret? How can you be a woman who takes their business to the next level?

The trick is not to ignore those feelings or try to shove them to the bottom of your mental drawer. It is not about shutting yourself down until they go away. There's a better way. Instead, let yourself experience those feelings to the fullest. Let yourself feel the range of emotions, as negative as you might perceive them to be. There are no "bad" or "good" emotions, just emotions you need to pay attention to and let out of your system.

I'll show you how to use the EBIQ Method to keep those down moments as short as possible, so you can regroup and refocus you energy, gain clarity and make your business vision a reality.

EBIQ Basics

Now, that you're aware of the "why," I want you start doing a few things that will help you break the isolation and build your support group. Isolation is the number one enemy of business owners, especially if you're a woman.

As women, we are wired to work in groups and help each other, and we are wired to live in tribes. The problem is the modern world is taking us further and further away from this way of life, and that leaves us confused, empty, and without a real support net. The EBIQ Method is about breaking this pattern and finding your "business tribe."

So how do you start connecting with people and building your tribe so you can take your business to the next level? First, you have to look around and find the people you can trust. That sounds easy, but, for many of us, trust can be a big issue, and we tend to stay away and save ourselves from getting hurt. So here's what I want you to do. Without this you won't be able to practice EBIQ, so get to work!

Start talking to other business owners and identify those who are *real* and willing to talk about how they feel as well as their failures.

Of course, you can always contact me and I will help you find a group, but you can also become an EBIQ Method certified leader and start a group in your area. For that, you will need to recruit people and find those who are ready to get real and use the tool.

The challenge of finding the right people is pretense—people, especially business owners, will not tell you about their challenges and will, usually, paint a picture of a better reality than they live. I've found that to be true in networking events; people will tell you they are doing very well, but when it comes to investing in themselves and their businesses—paying for coaching and other services—they never have enough money. To top that off, many people quit their new business within the first four years.

My goal, by writing this book and creating the EBIQ Method movement, is to start real conversations. In order to do that, you will need to practice showing vulnerability. The purpose of this exercise is to help you identify the people who will be a good fit as your EBIQ Method partners. Remember, the EBIQ Method is about using *emotions* to grow your business. You can't hide them anymore.

How to Start

I have a confession to make: I'm a personal-growth junkie. I read every self-help book I can get my hands on, and I hire coaches to help me grow my business and life. I practice mindset growth techniques daily, and my goal is to improve my life constantly.

Still, I spent many years searching for the missing link. Although I acquired many great tools that helped me change my life and grow my business, something was missing and I couldn't put my finger on what it was. I knew what I wanted to achieve—I had vision, I had clarity, and I knew what step to follow, but I wasn't ready for all the feelings that came up when I went to make my vision a reality.

Many people learn how to deny their emotions; it's a survival tool. We all know how to do it. We convince ourselves we are not scared, we are not confused, and we feel great about doing new things that are completely out of our comfort zone, although we have never done them before.

How do I know that? Because I, too, mastered denying my emotions. I was so good at lying to myself about how I felt that I almost believed myself. I was so good at it that I was able to graduate college completely disconnected from my family (my parents lived in a different country back then) while working crazy hours to support myself (my parents couldn't pay for my higher education) and while ignoring how isolated, lonely, and unsupported I felt. I spent hours in my tiny apartment, stressing out about money, dealing with a broken heart, missing my family, and there was no one there to assure me that everything would be fine, or simply let me cry on their shoulder while hugging me.

To graduate I had to lie to myself, otherwise I would not have been able to deal with the range of emotions that threatened to put me down. Little did I know that I could use those emotions to grow my life. Little did I know that by trying to ignore the emotions I was only taking energy away from the important things I had to focus on—graduating and emerging into my own life. If only I'd known back then about managing feelings, then this period of my life would have been a happy one.

Although all this happened before I had a business, those

types of feelings come up whenever you try to achieve something big, whether it's graduating college or starting a business. Whenever you try new things and set up big goals, big feelings will show themselves, and you'll need to deal with them.

So how do you manage the ups and downs of being a business owner? One day you're on top of the world after getting a phone call from Amazon asking you to be on their panel, and the next month you didn't sign up any new clients and feel like a total failure. This is exactly why I created the EBIQ, so you'll be able to move mountains, move mental and physical obstacles out of your way, and get to the finish line with ease.

In order to start using this tool I ask that you pay attention to your feelings for two days. Simply write down all the feelings that come up and what triggered them. This is a great place to start to get in touch with your emotions. It's not about doing anything with those feelings, not just yet, but it's about practicing paying attention to them and identifying their source.

Action Items

We are almost ready to dive into the nitty-gritty of the EBIQ, and I want you to have a few action items in hand. This will give you good idea of how to move forward and will help you create a change in your business and life.

1. Your feelings are your compass.

I want you to start looking at your feelings as a compass rather than an obstacle. We all experience feelings, and there's a reason why we are created with emotions at all. Feelings are there to help us tell right from wrong, to help us identify how to act, and to help us release emotional "baggage" that doesn't serve us.

If you are upset because your business didn't do so well last month and you're not sure where your next client will come from, you know that you need to think outside of the box, change your tactics, or act differently. You see, feeling upset is your compass. It shows you the way. It's your lodestar.

The problem is that we often mistake feeling bad as an obstacle, rather than our compass guiding us, and we end up wasting precious time being mad at ourselves for feeling that way.

I'll show you how to use that "negative" emotion (I

don't believe in negative or positive emotions, just simple, pure emotions) to gain clarity, recharge, and grow your business.

2. It's not about dwelling in misery and pain.
There's one thing I want to be clear about. This technique isn't about dwelling in misery and pain. Yes, you might feel pain, and yes, you might feel miserable, but the EBIQ Method is about how to take this range of emotions and turn them into a positive experience and growth.

The things I'm about to teach you might sound counterintuitive, scary, or even ridiculous at first, but that's only because they go against the grain, against everything you were taught and the messages you received since a very young age.

The EBIQ Method is about letting yourself feel any emotion to the fullest, releasing it by using your natural healing mechanism, and giving you a clear and rational thinking process so you can grow your business with ease.

What is the "natural healing and growth mechanism" I'm talking about? We are all born with the ability to release feelings, get rid of the emotional charge, and move on with our lives, recharged, as if nothing happened. Releasing the emotional charge of a hurt (which could be either physical or emotional) allows us to look at the same situation through different glasses. A release happens through uninterrupted cry, laughter, being angry, shaking, and more.

The idea is that we are built to release hurts and as proof you can look at young children—something happens, they cry/throw a tantrum/yell, and after a while they go back to their happy and content self and move on as if nothing happened. They feel connected to themselves and to the people around them and ready to try new things.

Here's a simple explanation: **Hurt → Release → Growth**

Diane is a dance teacher who owns a small dance studio. Her students love her and the business is growing slowly. One day, during an argument, her husband told her she would never be able to support herself because she was not a "smart business owner." Naturally, Diane was hurt by those words and couldn't think about anything else for two days. She blamed herself for "not being serious and smart" and spent a lot of time dwelling in her misery.

When we got together I simply listened to her and encouraged her to notice how mad and hurt she was. Holding that space allowed her to burst into tears and release the hurt. I also suggested she hit a pillow to let all the anger out, and she did—she hit it as hard as she could, while cursing and yelling.

When she was done she noticed that what her husband had said played into her insecurities and matched her self-talk, and therefore paralyzed her. By releasing the feelings she was trying to hold in she was able to get a fresh perspective and realize that she was far from being a failure. Not only that, she realized that her art brings joy to people's lives and that was her goal in the first place.

Identifying her true goals following the emotional release brought her growth and clarity, which is what we're after.

Chapter Summary

1. Big feelings come up when we're going after big goals. They are trying to keep us "safe."
2. Feelings are our inner compass. They are there for our higher good.
3. We are born with a natural healing mechanism that allows us to release tension and gain clarity.

Action Item

- Start an "Emotions journal." Whenever you feel stuck, identify the emotion that lies beneath the "stuckness" and write it down. Feeling stuck or bored is always a cover for something deeper.

CHAPTER 5: Listen and Be Heard (Intentional Listening)

This chapter lays the foundation for the EBIQ. This is the base upon which the whole system is laid. Learning how to listen in an intentional way will allow you, and your EBIQ Method partners, to release emotional charge to promote your growth.

Listening might sound easy, and it is a built-in mechanism we all have, but so few of us know how to listen in a way that allows for emotional release and growth. Most of us can't listen for more than 30 seconds without having the urgent need to interrupt. It's not that we want to interrupt, but most of us have never been listened to. So, whenever we have the chance to talk about ourselves, or to "fix" something, we can't hold back and we jump into the conversation, even if the only thing the other person was trying to do was let out emotion for growth. By interrupting the other person's talk and the releasing process, we prevent them from growing.

It's so important to develop your listening ability and spend time practicing it, so you can both listen well and be listened to.

I recommend finding a partner to practice the process—it will allow you faster learning of the tool. If you don't have one, make a decision to listen to people when they talk, without saying a word, unless they have asked you to speak. I would like you to find a partner because I want you to have the opportunity to be heard. That way you will learn how to access your emotions in order to release the charge.

The Power of Being Heard

When was the last time you were heard without interruptions? I mean, when was the last time someone sat next to you and listened to you without making any comments or suggestions on how to "fix" the problem you had? And when was the last time you wished they wouldn't interrupt, so you could be heard?

You've probably never had a conversation with someone where you listened to each other without interrupting the thought process at least one time. If you are lucky and you have, you know that by speaking uninterrupted, you are able to regain clear thinking and achieve the mental and emotional space necessary to take on new projects.

The idea behind the listening process is that we all have

the answers within us. We know what we want and we know what we need to do, but there are certain things holding us back that we need to "get out of our system."

The things holding us back have roots in our past—they are usually beliefs that were introduced to us by our parents and society and our past experiences. Those beliefs and experiences shaped the way we perceive the world and act as a "guide." We tend to make new decisions based on old experiences and rules that were true once and helped us in the past, but might not be the perfect solution to our present situation. That's where the problem lies.

We act based on decisions we made a long time ago and force the same solution upon a new situation.

When Emily was very young her parents worked long hours, and she was often left home alone. Back then, child-protection laws were not as advanced as they are today and this was common. One evening, when it was starting to get dark outside and the wind was howling, she was so scared she sat on the floor next to her bed, hugging a pillow and covering her ears. She had no idea when her parents would be back, and there was no one to comfort and protect her. She was only five and had no way of comforting herself.

This experience, and other experiences she had, made her believe that she was all alone in this world and that help was unavailable. She grew up taking care of herself, finding solutions and never asking for help. She developed "help blindness" and couldn't recognize help even when it was right in front of her.

When Emily's business started to grow to the point she couldn't do everything by herself anymore, she got stuck. As smart as she was, the "help blindness" prevented her from seeing that help was available and from asking for it. When we met, she was confused and couldn't figure out why she was stuck.

So I listened to her. I let her talk so she could process her thoughts and feelings. I didn't interrupt but was there for her, listening with full attention. I trusted Emily to have the answers and to figure out why she was stuck. The only question I asked her was, "When was the first time you felt that you were all by yourself?"

That was when she told me her story and started crying.

She talked and cried for about 30 minutes before she quieted, took a deep breath, and looked at me. At that moment, a lightbulb went off for her; she could tell the difference between her past experiences and her current situation. She knew she wasn't that young girl anymore and that, although feeling alone, help was out there and all she needed to do was ask for it.

Being heard and allowed to process her feelings and thoughts helped Emily to reevaluate the situation, get rid of old decisions, and look at the reality through clearer glasses. Emily reached out for help—she hired a team of freelancers to streamline her business, and all because she was heard.

Time Exchange

This next part might make you uncomfortable. Read this part once, then read it again and if it bothers you, ask yourself, "Why?"

This method of exchanging listening time and "using a time keeper" is different than what we experience when we talk to each other outside of EBIQ Method groups. It's very different from what we were taught, especially as women, that we need to listen to someone for as long as they need to talk, and it's different because it feels artificial. At least, in the beginning, until we get used to it.

The purpose of time exchange is to allow each person to listen and then talk without interruptions, so they can gain their rational thinking to grow their business. It's about creating a safe zone where you know you'll be listened to, and when you listen it won't be forever. It's about protecting you and your EBIQ Method partner by creating a framework that keeps both of you safe and allows you to have full attention from the other person.

So how do we do this, and what are the guidelines?

1. **Split the time equally**.
When you meet with your EBIQ Method partner for the weekly listening partnership meeting, each EBIQer gets the exact same time-chunk as the other person to be listened to. That means that if you have one hour, each one will get 30 minutes—no more and no less. Both of you will give and get the same.

At times you might feel you want to give more because the other person needs it more than you do, and that's why this is such an important rule to follow—most women are trained to give rather than receive, and it feels natural to us. But when we give and give without receiving we get upset, we feel victimized, and we start operating from the exact same place that got us stuck at the start. This rule is for you to practice contradicting your own patterns (those that hold you back from growing your business and life), and to make sure you won't pull yourself into "familiar" zones because they feel safe. This is about breaking old patterns by being listened to, and that's why I need to make sure you get as much as you give.

2. Set up a timer.

This is probably the most counterintuitive part of time exchange, because it feels artificial and we never do it, or almost never outside of EBIQ. Trust me though—this is what will keep you and your EBIQ Method partner from losing focus while listening to the other person.

So this is how it goes: first you need to decide how much time each person gets—let's say each one of you will listen for 15 minutes and then will be listened to for 15 minutes. Now you need to set up the timer for exactly 15 minutes.

Once the timer goes off the person who's being listened to knows their time is up and needs to end their session. This means they need to stop talking or stop the releasing process.

If the timer went off when that person was talking or releasing emotions, they can take an extra minute or so to finish the thought or pull themselves together. The important thing is that they know the conversation ends, and now it's their turn to listen. The difference from other "conversations" is that once the time is up, instead of going home it's your turn to listen to the other person.

You see, the timer protects you from the need to listen forever to the other person. In real life when someone starts talking we never know when it's going to end, and we lose patience after a short while. More than that, because we're more likely not to be heard, we bring up our own issues whenever possible. For example, a conversation might go like this:

> **Danny**: *You have to hear what happened to me yesterday. My boss, who I hate, told me I need to improve or I'll go home. I feel so bad, and I don't know what to do. I'm so lost. I cried last night, and I can't stop thinking that I will never find a new job. [Danny needs someone to listen to him so he can process what happened, how he feels about it, and what next step to take.]*
>
> **Amanda** *(who thinks this rant might go forever): This happened to me last month too, and, you know what, I still feel so bad... [She goes on about her own experience.]*

You see, Amanda wasn't really listening; she was looking for the first chance to talk about her own experience because she never had the chance to process it, and she assumes she won't be heard by Danny once he's done—which is a realistic assumption. That's why the timer rule is so handy and keeps the EBIQ Method relationship in place—you get what you give and vice versa.

Once you know there's a time frame and you won't need to listen forever, your mind is not occupied with "when will this person stop talking" and you can listen with full intention and concentration. Also, you know you'll be listened to by the other person when your turn comes.

3. Emotional Release.*

The purpose of the time exchange is to help you release emotions and therefore advance your business and life. Emotional release has many forms and each form helps release a different emotion. Although we use all of the emotional release forms naturally, we rarely get to have a full release because we're being interrupted. Later on I will discuss how to help one release their emotions and what to say (or what not to say) in order to support that process.

Meanwhile I want you to be clear about some of the forms of emotional release:

- Crying—releases sadness, hurt, grief
- Laughing—releases embarrassment
- Shaking—releases fear
- Sweating—releases fear, tension

*You can read more about the forms of emotional release on page xxx [The Emotional Release Chart]

4. Gain your rational thinking.

But why is emotional release so important to my business growth process?

Well, this is the key to getting rid of all the parts that block you from playing big and trying new things. It's about doing some deep inner cleaning and throwing away what doesn't serve you anymore. And it's about re-evaluating your actions, where they come from, how they serve or disserve you, and coming up with a plan.

Here's another example. When Sheryl worked with me on writing her book so she could become a leader in her field, she often got stuck and didn't know what to write about. Sheryl is a bright woman in her 50s who's achieved many things in her life—she's great at her job and raised three happy and successful kids. She is active in her local community and the go-to person when someone needs help.

Sheryl's goal was to package all her knowledge in a book so more people would get the help they needed. She had a process she used over and over again with her patients, and she wanted to grow her business to reach even more people.

But Sheryl got scared.

The book was a few steps away from being completed, and Sheryl couldn't bring herself to write another word. In our weekly meeting I asked her, "What could happen when this book is published?" and her answer was, "I'll be ridiculed." This is a funny answer because published authors are well respected and publishing a book is a big achievement, but Sheryl couldn't see that—she was caught in her old experiences that revolved around ridicule.

So I asked her another question, "When was the first time you felt that way?" It took her a while but then a memory popped up—she was reading her essay in front of her whole class in middle school and some kids made fun of her idea and it made her feel ashamed.

Sheryl told me she was very proud of her essay, and was very excited to read it in front of the class. She practiced reading it in front of the mirror for two days, and felt confident. As she was reading it to the class she was proud of herself and expected her classmates would appreciate the essay and the effort she had put into it. Although she got an A+, her classmates, most of them boys, started calling her names such "smartass," and said things like "Sheryl thinks she's so smart" and, "Who do you think you are—Einstein?" It made Sheryl feel that showing her knowledge not only separated her from other kids, but put her in the center with all the poison arrows directed at her. Not only did she want to hide but she also didn't know why they were treating her that way. She was humiliated for something she was proud of doing.

Although that was a long time ago, the hurt was still there and she started crying. Once she was done, she was able to see that although there's a similarity between reading your essay in front of the class and publishing a book, it is also very different—she's older now and can protect herself and manage her own feelings, not to mention she has a process that is proven to help people—she's an expert!

Once Sheryl released the emotional block, she went back to writing and the book was done within less than a month.

You see, our mental pipes are clogged because of past experiences and the way to unclog them is to release the emotions attached to our old experiences. Once we do that we can move forward full force. We release the emotions and, by doing so, gain our rational thinking that allows us to act on our goals and grow our business and life.

Chapter Summary

1. A listening partnership is the key to healing yourself from past hurts so you can grow your life and business.
2. A timer is the tool that keeps the listening partnership from going sour—it helps set up boundaries and make sure you get as much as you give.
3. Emotional release is the "missing link" between knowing what to do and acting on it.
4. Releasing old hurts will allow you to gain rational thinking and grow your business and life.

Action Item

- Practice intentional listening. Either find a partner, or practice listening to people without interrupting them at all. Remember, this is about developing *your* intentional listening abilities.

Ally Nathaniel

CHAPTER 6: What to Do When the "Stuff" Hits the Fan

Why do we feel the way we do and how does it stop us from growing?

More often than not we are led by our feelings. We act from a very deep and mostly unaware place inside ourselves—an irrational place. We all want to believe that all the decisions we make are based on a rational thinking process, but over and over again it has been proven that, unless we are aware of our feelings, we act from our heart rather than our brain. What I mean by that is we react to a situation from an "instinctive" place rather than a logical place.

This instinctive place is where we store our early and past experiences—the experiences that shaped who we are and taught us how to operate in this world. But what worked for us in the past, when we were children and even after, might not be the best solution for present situations. Think about Emily who operated from a place of loneliness and was not able to ask for help because she believed help was not available—this is operating based on feelings rather than rational thinking and rational decision-making processes.

Operating from this place will sabotage your business growth. That's why you're looking for answers. Most times it stops you from trying new things and playing big, but sometimes your early programing will make you act before thinking or take action before sketching the map. In both cases your business growth will suffer, either from staying in place or making rash decisions that might destroy your business.

Don't get me wrong, I'm not saying not to act and not to try new things. All I'm saying is you need to make sure to look at any situation rationally. In order to do that, you might need to release emotional blocks and set free old patterns.

Claim Your Intelligence First

We are intelligent creatures. We are born intelligent, and we have the ability to evaluate situations and respond to them in an "intelligent" way. What I mean by "intelligent" is that unlike other animals that use reflexes and conditioned responses, we have the ability to produce a unique and specific response to each situation.

When we bump into a situation at work, in our family, or with friends, our unique advantage as humans is that we have the ability to evaluate what it is we need to do and react differently even if the situation is similar.

For example, you will act differently if your mom asks you to get her a glass of water than if a complete stranger on the street asks you to do the same. Although the situation has similarities—in both cases someone asks you to serve them a glass of water—your intelligence allows you to tell the differences and therefore choose a correct response. Your mom will get a glass of water right away, no question asked, but with the stranger you might ask questions or walk away.

You see, your response is based on the situation, the whole picture rather than a simple stimulation and reaction–this is what I call intelligent.

The EBIQ Method is all about releasing emotional blocks in order to reclaim our intelligence so we can respond better to situations.

Old Stuff Feels "Real"—Your Patterns

So why is it so hard to simply look at a situation, evaluate, and react based on the data? Why is it so hard to operate from a rational place? Why do we regret saying or doing something we shouldn't have done or said? Well, it's so hard because we are human and we tend to apply what worked for us in the past to present situations, even if they are only slightly similar to each other. By the way, this isn't only about action, but about how we feel when stuff happens. And once our emotions are activated, it's difficult to think rationally.

I call it reactivation, and this is the state when feelings arise as a result of an event. If we pay close attention to the situation and the feeling it activated, we will notice that if the situation was similar enough to something that happened to us in the past, it re-activated the same sensations and, often, responses.

For example, let's say your dad used to yell at you, call you names, and humiliate you. He had a specific tone of voice he used when he acted this way. This tone of voice scared you so much your body would get all tense and your heart rate sped up. These physical reactions became your pattern—every time your father did that, you would act that way automatically, without thinking about it. The tone of voice and the physical reaction became tangled.

You see, our brains link information and feeling—we remember better when there's an emotion attached. That's why memories come to life vividly, as if they just happened, when our senses and emotions are engaged.

Here is an example of reactivation:

I love to bake, and my banana bread is to die for—if I do say so about myself, haha. When I met my friend Tammi I brought her a slice of the bread. The minute she opened the box and the smell hit her nostrils, a tear trickled down her cheek. When I asked her what happened she said that her mom, who passed away a few months earlier, used to bake the same banana bread. The smell reminded her of her mom and she was yearning to hold her hand again.

In this example, the smell (situation) reactivated an emotion (yearning). This is exactly what happens to us in various situations. We need to call people and offer our services, but calling people reminds us of trying to raise money for a cause in elementary school and people rejecting our offer or hanging up on us. We felt humiliated and confused.

Calling strangers to offer our services is similar enough to the original experience so it re-activates the old feelings (humiliation and confusion) and that blocks us from taking action. Thus, we are stuck.

A tone of voice, the look of a person, or even body language can be a trigger to reactivating emotions and blocking us from thinking rationally and operating accordingly. And at that moment it's very hard to tell the difference between reality and the feelings that are reactivated, which belong to a different, and usually old, experience.

The aspiration is to act rationally, always, to use our full intelligence and eliminate any setbacks or stalls by releasing the patterns creating the emotional tangle and our paralysis.

This is where the EBIQ Method comes in—it allows you to track the origins of the feeling, release the emotions that got you stuck, and approach the situation in a rational way that will allow you to achieve your goals with ease.

Recognize The Source, Eliminate the Block

So how do you reclaim your rational thinking so you can approach any situation with your eyes wide open and evaluate it based on data rather than feelings?

The first step is to locate the source of what's blocking your pipeline and preventing you from being rational, creative, and willing to take on new challenges. This source is always a *feeling* that got tangled with an unpleasant past experience in a way that's stopping you from taking action.

When using intentional listening with each other, the

purpose is to identify that source (the original experience and the feeling accompanying the experience) and contradict it in a way that will allow emotional release. Identifying the source is the diagnosis, and the emotional release is the cure. Identifying by itself is not enough, even though it can bring relief, and releasing will occur only when you've identified the source and how it's different from your current circumstance.

In order to recognize the source, we need access our past, which is not always easy, especially when we're confronting an uncomfortable experience or feeling. Most people will do anything in their power to stay away from that hurt—they have no desire to go back and re-experience it.

I want to be very clear on one thing: If you see the value of the EBIQ Method and want to use this tool to accomplish big things and grow your business, you will have to be willing to confront those feelings and experiences, so you can release the emotional charge attached to them.

So how do you recognize the source of the block? How do you get to the root of your patterns so you can change them?

You have to be willing to do the work. You have to decide to give this process a chance and follow the instructions.

Practice using intentional listening with a partner. This partner can be someone who's a member of one of the EBIQ Method groups, or you can teach someone the principles. The important thing is that the two of you will be clear on what you're trying to achieve and speak the same language (see glossary).

There are some questions you can use to help your listening partner access their unconscious parts, which are covered by layers of protection built over the years. Under those layers you'll find the answers that will help release the emotional blocks.

Feeling Identification Techniques

What is it that you need to ask each other to gain access to those hidden places where the feelings are hidden? Let's go over three simple techniques you can use when listening to someone, to help them locate the earliest moment that is the core of the impediment, false perspective, or incompetent feeling they're experiencing.

1. **Use "flash answers."**
This technique requires that you trust the human mind has the capability to come up with accurate information within a fraction of a second. Whatever comes up is what you need to

focus on, even if it looks unrelated or if it "doesn't make sense." If you follow your mind it will lead you to where you need to be and what you need to work on.

A flash answer can be given to a question such as:

"When was the first time you felt that way?" or "Who does this person remind you of?" The first thing that comes to mind is most important.

I want to remind you that the purpose of getting in touch with these feelings is to release them.

2. Slow down.

Many times we hide our emotions by being overactive. We take on extra tasks, make ourselves available to our family and friends without setting boundaries, volunteer in ten different organizations, and never say "no" to anything. These behavioral patterns serve us because they don't allow us to rest. When we're occupied 26 hours a day we don't have time to pay attention to what's really going on inside us and to connect with our feelings.

When feeling stuck, we need to gain access to those feelings to release them. Therefore, slowing down is a great technique to use.

If someone speaks a lot without pausing for breath, you can suggest they "breathe and slow down." This is usually enough for them to start releasing emotion. If they keep talking you can put you hand on their shoulder, look them in the eye and state, "Slow down."

3. **Distinguish reality from feelings.**

In the story about Emily, she *felt* as if help was unavailable to her. Based on her past experience of not having support, she grew up to believe this was true. Once she could tell the difference between now and then—"back then I was little and had no way of knowing help was available if my parents were not around," vs. "I can *ask for help* and there are many people who will be willing to assist me, and I can also pay for help"—she was able to take action. The feelings paralyzed her, even though they had nothing to do with what was possible for her in present day.

You see, Emily was able to distinguish her feelings (that were rooted in the past) from what's available to her today. Based on that, she was able to get the help she needed to grow her business.

There are many other techniques that can be learned in the EBIQ Method course, but if you take those three examples you will achieve a lot of success. Please keep in mind that the purpose of using these techniques is to achieve emotional release, which can be laughter, tears, anger, and more. The emotional release itself is what you're after, and you need to trust the process to get yourself unstuck, allow yourself to take on things you weren't able to take on before, and therefore grow your business.

Chapter Summary

1. The key to growing your business is operating from a logical place, rather than from an instinctive place.
2. Intelligence is choosing the right response based on the situation, rather than using instinctive responses.
3. Behavioral patterns (reactions) and emotions are tangled. Present business experiences might trigger old memories and reactivate patterns.
4. In order to act from a rational place, we need to learn how to separate the experience from the memory and eliminate the pattern.
5. Identifying the source of the emotional block and releasing it is key to growing our business.

Action Item

- In your Emotional Journal create a new section called "My Core Experiences" and then use "flash answers" to identify your "stuckness" source. Ask yourself "when was the first time I felt that way," and write down what comes up. After a few days you will have a list of core experiences you can use for emotional release. These are the early experiences that shaped your patterns and perceptions.

CHAPTER 7: Contradictions

In previous chapters I touched a little bit on the things we can say to encourage our listening partner to discharge. Those things are called "contradictions," and I will use this chapter to tell you more about what they are and how they work.

What Are Contradictions?

Every setback pattern has its root in powerlessness. Whenever we feel powerless we are unable to take action, move forward, and grow our business. Powerlessness patterns have many forms and shapes, and they are particularly visible among women and oppressed minorities.

Although the reality is that the power was taken from those groups for many years, it is slowly coming back, at least in today's western world. Though there is still more work for people to do in every country to fight oppression and stigmas against women and minorities, those same women can often achieve more than they realize. But most of them still feel powerless and stay small because of past experiences. They identify themselves as victims and can't see a way out.

Many women hold those patterns and have a hard time releasing them. I have to admit that, although I take on powerful actions such as building a business, writing books, and coaching other women, I also have those setback patterns in me. I use the EBIQ Method to heal myself and release those patterns. They have such a strong hold on us that we need to pay full attention and dedicate time to eliminating them. The EBIQ Method is the tool that allows you to do that, but it takes commitment, willingness, and hard work.

So what can we do to help each other release the emotional tangle around setback patterns? How can we recognize that whatever feeling we experience in the moment is rooted in the past and can be eliminated if we recognize its origins and release the emotions tangled to it? We need to show the person we are helping that the emotion has nothing to do with current events, and it is all about old experiences and decisions made a long time ago. Once the person can tell the difference, they will naturally release emotions and work toward eliminating the setback pattern. This is done through saying or doing things that make it clear the feeling has nothing to do with the situation.

Here is an example. Helen has a small business where

she teaches families how to cook healthy food to support a healthy lifestyle. As she was growing her business she came across obstacles every business owner bumps into such as finding new clients, writing marketing materials and finding support. Helen felt overwhelmed. As if everything was too hard, and there was no way she'd be able to get over the obstacles and move her business forward. She needed more clients, and she felt powerless. She was caught deep in her false perspective and couldn't look beyond it.

As I was listening to her I asked, "What does this struggle remind you of?"

I asked her to give me a flash answer, and she immediately said, "My dad." She talked about how her dad, whom she loved deeply, struggled with his business. She looked up to him and wasn't able to help him since she was so young. She absorbed his pain, and that pain got tangled up with her powerlessness. At some point, her dad went bankrupt, and there was nothing she could do about it.

Being a struggling business owner was similar enough to that past experience. She needed to take action but couldn't because of the powerlessness she felt. My question allowed her to release all the anger and sadness inside her. During one session she hit pillows and yelled, "I want to help you, Dad," and in another session she kept saying, while crying, "I can't help you, I can't help you," while I held her. In another session she told me all the things she told herself when she couldn't help her father: "You're too young, you can't help," "You know nothing," and other messages she heard back then. Letting everything out and releasing the emotions allowed her to get back her clear mind, and from there she sat down and wrote a business plan that would allow her to acquire clients. She created new services and connected with new referral partners.

Using the EBIQ Method allowed Helen to eliminate her powerlessness patterns and regain her clear mind so she could focus on her business.

Physical/ Non-Verbal Contradictions

As adults we speak in order to process our thoughts and feelings—we talk to friends, to therapists, sometimes to strangers in a local bar. We use our verbal abilities to process our emotional hurdles and that works oftentimes. But there are so many other non-verbal ways that we can use to contradict the false perspective and show ourselves or our listening partner that their setback patterns are not real—they are just a thought that can be changed by releasing the emotion attached.

Physical contradictions show another person that we are

there, we hear them, and we are paying attention to them, which is, by itself, a big contradiction. Most of us never received the attention we craved growing up, and because of this lack of attention and support, we developed powerlessness setback patterns. Now we feel we can't achieve certain things or we can't do something, when the reality is that we have all the power in the world.

I want you to close your eyes for a second and think about how wonderful things could have been if only you had someone sitting and paying attention to you when you needed it. Someone who didn't judge you or instruct you to do things in a different way. Someone who saw you and was willing to support you with whatever you needed and let you lead the way.

I've spoken to many adolescents, and they've told me they would love their parents to sit next to them when times get tough—just being there with them is the support they need. Knowing that they are not alone gives them the power to move on, cope with difficult situations, and come up with new solutions. You see, the physical presence of the parents is a contradiction to the loneliness and isolation. Loneliness and isolation can produce powerlessness patterns and stop us from achieving big things. By contradicting those patterns, we can help a person release emotions so they can heal and go after their dreams and goals.

Here are some physical contradictions you can use to show your listening partner they are not alone:

1. **Hold their hand while listening to them**—Maintaining physical contact with your listening partner is a recommended practice. When we feel our partner, it's easier to notice we are not alone. For many people, isolation setback patterns are so strong it is hard for them to realize there's someone there with them. Since most of us have some level of isolation pattern, touching gently or holding hands while listening to each other will help the person digest the truth that feeling lonely is a setback pattern rather than a reality.

2. **Look them in the eyes**—Direct eye contact is a great contradiction not only for loneliness, but for embarrassment patterns as well. Many people avoid direct eye contact because of the intimacy it creates. Intimacy is something we practice with only a few people and try to avoid at all cost with others. There's much embarrassment around intimacy that can be released to help us grow. If you think about it, so many decisions we make are to avoid embarrassment. We limit our lives so we won't have to face embarrassment,

be ridiculed, or feel ashamed. Think of all the opportunities that will open up to you if you stop fearing those things—your power will be unlimited. Look your listening partner in the eye and help them release embarrassment so they can grow their life and business.

There are other non-verbal ways to contradict a false perspective, and you are welcome to be creative with that. Some other non-verbal contradictions are: facial expressions, a hug, making sounds, changing your tone of voice, and more.

Verbal Contradictions

There are many things you can say to show your listening partner their false perspective is rooted in the past and has nothing to do with present events. When they notice the gap they will release emotions and see reality in a much clearer way. Having this clarity will allow them to take action.

It is possible that your listening partner will try to argue with your contradictions, because that's what we're all trained to do—we argue because it doesn't feel good to do the opposite of what we're used to. We argue because the thought of trying something new (even if it's just in a session) is scary. We argue to keep ourselves "safe." This is why non-verbal contradictions are so important and why I recommend combining them with a verbal contradiction—we are less likely to argue with a tone of voice than with the content of the contradiction.

Things you can say:

1. **Direct statement** — *"You are not alone." "You are qualified to do that." "You've done harder things in the past."*

    These statements show the person that what they *feel* is different from reality.

2. **Understatements** — *"It sometimes happens that a woman is very successful in business." "It's happened that someone successfully achieved a goal she/he set."*

    These understatements take the focus off the person and allow them to see that their belief is a possible false perspective. It is easier for us to notice our own false perspective if someone else has done what we want to do and has succeeded. This way, it's easier for our brain to connect the dots and see that we're dealing with our own false perspective rather than reality. If something can be done by someone else, then it might be possible for us.

3. **Flash answers** — *"Who does this person remind you of?" "When was the first time you felt that way?"*
Flash answers allow us a direct contact with our unaware mind. If you trust your thinking and work on the first thing that comes up, I guarantee you will see the connection at some point, even if it didn't make sense at the beginning.

The feeling that comes up to me many times in my business and personal life is that if other people have succeeded in something, I can't be successful as well. It is as if there's not enough business for everyone. Every time I bump into competition I feel there's no point in building my business, and I should quit. Although I know it is a false perspective, and there's room for everyone, my false perspective is so strong that I argue with reality.

When my listening partner asked me, "When was the first time you felt that way?" My immediate answer was, "Always."

"But what does 'always' mean?" she asked. "Can you share a specific time frame?"

The picture that came to mind was of a baby lying in a

crib, and a strong notion of loneliness flooded my body. It took me a few seconds to realize that this baby was me. I was lying there in a crib in the babies' house in the Kibbutz, feeling lonely and isolated.

It might sound weird—there's no way I could remember that at such a young age—but this was the first image that came to mind, and I trusted it. I also believe that our cells remember everything and that we can access those memories using flash answers.

This notion of loneliness and isolation was the first time my little brain realized there's not enough love and attention for all the babies. We were six babies and had only two caregivers. If the caregiver was feeding or changing another baby, she wasn't able to pay attention to me. This was where the belief of not having enough resources for everyone started to grow. If another baby is getting what they need, there was no option I'd get it at the same time.

You see, I took a realization I'd made at a very young age and projected it on a situation I had in my adult life as a business owner. It took me many hours of releasing feelings of anger and sadness to accept that there's always enough room for everyone and competition will not take away from me. Not only that, competition can *help* me grow my business.

I want you to start using contradictions with yourselves

and with your listening partners to pin the moments when your setback patterns started to form. Remember, working early is the only way to attack and dissolve the feelings we experience when growing our business. It is almost always true that whatever you currently feel is a false perspective and rooted in your early days on this planet. Some people will say it is tied to your family history and beliefs, and I agree with that, but that's a discussion for another time.

Chapter Summary

1. Held-back patterns are a result of powerless thoughts that are rooted in our history
2. The EBIQ Method's purpose is to help you release held-back patterns, and it takes commitment on your end.
3. Contradictions are how we show our listening partner their held-back patterns are not real, so they can release them.
4. There are physical contradictions and verbal contradictions you can use in different situations.
5. The root of every held-back pattern is in your early days. In your listening partnership sessions work as early as possible.

Action Item

- As you practice using contradictions in your listening partnership, make sure to write down every contradiction that yields an emotional release. You can ask your listening partner to use a contradiction that worked in the past over and over again until you have completely released the early hurt.

CHAPTER 8: Rejections and Excuses

The concept behind the EBIQ Method is that once you place your full attention on a specific area and release the emotions that are blocking you from taking big steps forward, you will be able to advance yourself and your business in ways that were not available to you before.

I want you to be clear about the process: first, you use intentional listening to identify a setback pattern and the emotion attached to it. In order to identify the pattern and emotion, you use the techniques discussed in the previous chapter. Once identified, it's time to release the emotion using your natural healing mechanisms such as crying, laughter, tantrums, screaming, and others.

While releasing the emotions, your only concern is to stay in the moment and release as much as possible. Your listening partner is there to help you release even more. Their job is to say things or ask questions that will keep the releasing process going. The challenge in keeping this process going is that we are trained to keep our emotions in at all costs, and it's very hard to go against the grain. You'll need to trust me and my clients' experience that this works. This is why finding a listening partner you can trust is important—it will allow you to release emotions more easily, knowing they're trustworthy. Trust will grow with time, so find a partner you're comfortable with, practice the EBIQ Method with them while following the confidential rules, and you'll be fine.

> Your job is to stay in the moment and release as much emotion as possible.

The challenge is to train your brain to believe this type of behavior is acceptable. This means that you will need to adopt new beliefs and delete the old ones. For example, you can tell yourself that crying is good and you shouldn't stop until you're out of tears instead of "get yourself together." Your listening partner's job is to encourage you to keep releasing until the timer goes off. They can say certain things to keep the release process going:

- "Stay there, keep releasing."
- "Let's go back to [whatever it is that helped them release]." For example, "Let's go back to when you were a little baby lying in the crib."

- "Keep going, it's OK, this is exactly what you need to be doing."

Your job as the listening partner is to put the other person back on track to release the emotional blocks.

> Your job as the listening partner is to put the other person back on track to release the emotional blocks.

Rejection

As a business owner, you probably know that being rejected is simply a part of the process. You offer your products or services, and many people say no. You want to connect with influencers in your field, and they are not interested. You probably hear "no" more often than "yes" on a regular basis.

Although hearing "no" is part of the process, it can reactivate old feelings and bring your false perspective to the surface. Once your false perspective is in an operation mode, it is very hard to tell the difference between reality and your old feelings.

I love working on rejection because most of us have

been rejected at one point or another. Some of us as babies, others in school, but our first experience with rejection always goes back in time, way back, and it is relatively easy to remember when everything started.

The purpose of working on feelings of rejection is that you can reach out for new opportunities in your business and you won't get confused when getting rejected. If you release enough feelings that are tied up to rejection experiences, you'll be able to try over and over again, reach out to people, and make endless offers to potential clients. You won't take *any* rejection personally.

Saying "NO"

Saying "no" is hard, especially for women. Our social training is to placate others—to take care of the needs and feelings of the people around us. We are trained to be "good girls" and to be "nice," so it's no wonder saying "no" is not our strong suit. Good girls don't say "no"—they do what they are asked to do. Nice girls don't say "no," otherwise they won't be considered nice anymore.

The results of not acting as expected can be harsh—you

might be punished, physically or emotionally, and in both cases you'll be humiliated. While boys who say "no" might be considered assertive or courageous, this is not the case for girls. Of course, boys can be punished for saying "no" as well—this is where adultism kicks in; a child is not allowed to say no to an adult—but girls get constant messages about behaving the right way, being respectful and delicate, and saying "no" simply won't get them there. Saying "no" is about standing up for yourself, knowing what you want, and expressing it. As women, we all need to practice saying "no" more often.

When you work on saying "no" in your listening partnership time, I suggest saying it to all the things you didn't want to do as a child. It might cause you to laugh or get angry, or you might feel sad. No matter what it is, let it out and keep releasing for as long as possible, until the timer goes off.

Things you can say:
- "I don't want to eat that."
- "I'm not cleaning my room."
- "I'm not kissing Uncle Joe."

Say What You Want

Another option, which provides great practice for women, is to state what you want. Not only are we discouraged from saying "no," but we are also discouraged from vocalizing what we want. Saying what you want is being fully connected with yourself and being clear on what feels good and what doesn't. It's about voicing your thoughts and putting yourself in the center—something most females were taught is not OK.

When I speak to girls and women they often answer, "I don't know," to simple questions such as, What do you want to eat? What do you want to do? Who's your favorite singer? Even my daughter acts that way. I remember myself saying that many times, especially as a teenager and a young adult. It wasn't that I didn't know what I wanted—I was afraid to express it. Life experience taught me that if I said it out loud I would probably be ridiculed or ashamed, or simply told it's nonsense.

You see, I internalized that saying what I want will only cause trouble, so I stopped saying it. That's why I got stuck with a boyfriend I didn't love for two years when I was only 15, and that's why my job was to work in children's houses when I was a teenager even though I hated it. I was afraid of stating what I wanted because good girls think of themselves last.

I want you to start practicing saying what you want, or

what you don't want and be very clear about it:
- "I want to have sex now."
- "I don't want to have sex tonight."
- "I want to help women find the love they deserve."
- "I want to be the president of the United States."
- "I have no intention of losing weight."

Come up with your own statements and take them into a listening partnership session. Try different statements and figure out which ones have the most emotional charge, then release it. Remember to get to work on this as early as possible—if you release the early emotional block, its effect in the present will lessen.

Repeat the same statement over and over again for as long as it helps with the releasing process. If you are the listener, encourage your partner to repeat the statements that produce the most emotional release.

Asking for Help

Asking for help is crucial for business growth. Help could come from a friend or someone you compensate for their time. The thing is, help is always available, and it is just your false perspective that prevents you from seeing it. Once the emotional block is released, you'll see help everywhere.

Work on early times in your life when you couldn't find help.

For Erica, it was when she was four years old. Her family was involved in a car accident and her parents lost consciousness and died shortly after. Experiencing such a traumatic event at such a young age left Erica hurt, confused, and afraid. Since she didn't have any relatives who could take care of her, she was put into an orphanage and moved between foster families. For years she was looking for help but couldn't find it. Erica was one of my listening partners, and she spent hours and hours working on disappointment, powerlessness, and fear.

Although she did not believe help was available, releasing the hurt allowed her to see that help *is* available. It took her a long time, but setting up a goal to look out for people who can help and ask for their assistance finally paid off.

Releasing false perspectives can take time, especially if they are rooted in early childhood. Trusting the process is the key to success. If you release enough emotional blocks, you will look at reality through crystal clear glasses and notice things you didn't before.

Excuses

How many times have you found yourself making excuses as to why you can't do this or that?

Many of us confuse a reason with an excuse because we tend to rationalize excuses. We convince ourselves that there's a valid reason as to why we can't achieve a goal while others can. I'm the last person to tell you there aren't reasons—for some people achieving a goal will be much harder than for others because of life circumstances.

For example, if you're a mom who's the main caregiver, it will be harder for you to work 12 hours a day in an office compared to someone who doesn't have kids. Not having as much time as someone who doesn't have kids is not an excuse, but a reality.

In saying that, if you want to achieve something, you can organize your life around it. You might need to make some changes, and you might need to stand up for yourself or change your mindset, but it is possible. Making changes can be scary as hell, and that fear is what causes us to rationalize our excuses and call them "reasons." Whenever I wasn't able to achieve something in my life, whether in my business or personal life, it always came down to fear—a fear that I might fail, a fear that I might succeed, or a fear of upsetting someone. It doesn't matter what it was; it was always about me holding myself back. Releasing the emotions that were attached to the fear allowed me to take the next step and ultimately achieve my goal. This is what the EBIQ Method is all about.

I want you to be honest with yourself when looking into excuses. Most times powerlessness patterns are involved, and it's your job to release these emotional blocks. Powerlessness patterns are huge obstacles for many women—after all, our power was taken away from us for many years, and for many women, this is still going on today. Internalized powerlessness patterns are what is left inside us from that ongoing oppression, and it takes awareness and effort to release them.

If you're having a hard time letting go of those patterns, ask yourself, "What do I benefit from holding on to them?" "How do they serve me?" Many times we profit from our patterns on a subconscious level, and admitting that will help you contradict the pattern and release the emotional charge.

An Example

Elena was an independent woman who made a good living before marrying her husband. Everything changed when her first child was born. Suddenly, she was expected to stay home with her child even though that wasn't her plan. Caught by surprise, it took Elena a couple of years to admit to herself this was not what she wanted. During that time, she rationalized her situation by convincing herself that this was the right thing to do, that it was the best thing for her child, and that mothers are natural caregivers and therefore should stay home. All of those reasons didn't feel right to Elena, but she kept going.

After two years, she felt she couldn't do it anymore. She wanted her previous life back. She want to be both a mom and a professional woman who could support herself, so she brought it up with her husband, expecting him to jump in and offer to share parental duties. His reaction caught her by surprise once again—he wanted her to stay home. He even got upset she'd suggested going back to work.

At that point, it took a lot of courage on Elena's end to stand up for herself and be clear about what she needed. His reaction was not what she'd expected and she knew if she pushed it they would end up fighting, so she brought it to a listening partnership session and released the fear.

You see, the fear could have stopped her, and she could have said to herself that staying home was the right thing to do, which would have been a rationalization. But she chose to confront her husband instead. After all, they were a team and cared for each other. She came up with a plan. Although her husband got upset—he'd need to take on more responsibilities at home if she got a job—she was able to stay grounded and fight for herself. The fear was released, so she grasped the life she wanted and figured out a balance between caring for her child and pursuing her career.

Chapter Summary

1. The EBIQ Method summary: Use intentional listening to identify a setback pattern and the emotion attached to it. In order to identify the pattern and emotion, use the techniques discussed in the previous chapter. Once identified, it's time to release the emotion using your natural healing mechanisms such as crying, laughter, tantrums, screaming, and more.
2. Your job is to stay in the moment and release as much emotion as possible.
3. Your job as the listening partner is to put the other person back on track to release the emotional blocks.
4. Practice saying "no "and asking for what you want to activate the release process.
5. Excuses are rationalizations of fear.

Action Item

- Practice saying "no" to things that are distracting you from working toward achieving your goals, both professional and personal. Start by saying "no" to small things and then progress to bigger ones.

Ally Nathaniel

CHAPTER 9: Decide, Act, Release

But how do you take action when you're scared? Where do you find the courage to stand up for yourself, to do something you've never done before, to change the rules? How do you do that when you're paralyzed by fear, when you feel the world will turn upside down if you take action? How do you order your brain to take the first step when you know the journey you're about to start will be uncomfortable?

In this chapter, I will answer those questions and show you how to use the EBIQ Method to overcome the barriers, fears, and doubts holding you back. You will learn how to use the EBIQ Method to differentiate your setback patterns from reality, so you'll see how powerful and unstoppable you are. You'll have a new perception about who you are and how to use your powers to grow your business. Perception is the key, and by using the EBIQ, you will see reality as it is—always in your favor.

It's All About the Feelings

I know some people get upset when I tell them the only thing stopping them from achieving what they want is them—their thoughts, feelings, and actions. That the only thing standing in their way to being as big as they want and growing their business is their early experiences that created a belief system.

Many of us feel we have no control over our thoughts, but that's not true. Not only can we control our thoughts; we can choose those thoughts that serve us and help us grow, rather than those that keep us small. It is up to you to choose the thoughts that serve you, so you can achieve any goal you set and grow your business and life.

I suggest you take the limiting thoughts you have into a listening partnership session and look into them, read them out loud, find contradictions to them, and rehearse saying them to achieve emotional release.

For example:

1. If your thought is, "I don't know enough to call myself an expert," you can contradict it by asking your listening partner to say, "If you can say 'I'm an expert' that makes you an expert." This will probably make you giggle, realizing that you know more than you give yourself

credit for. Laughing at something is one of the emotional release forms and that's what you're after—releasing emotions to allow yourself to see reality as it is.

2. Take some time to write down your limiting beliefs. Start with the beliefs that you think are stopping you from growing your business and make a list of them. The best way to do this is in a quiet room where you can connect to the flow of thoughts. Start by asking yourself, "What do I believe in that's stopping me from being as big as I want?" Write down everything that comes to mind. Trust that this is what needs to come out, even if it doesn't make sense at the moment.

3. Once you're done, highlight three to four sentences that strike you as the core of your beliefs and copy them to a new list. Now, take some more time to come up with contradictions—sentences that are the opposite of your core beliefs that you'll use in a listening partnership session.

4. In the session read them out loud and let yourself *feel* them. Everything we say or think generates feelings, because feelings are thoughts in motion.

The EBIQ Method is all about connecting to your feelings—they are the key to achieving success in business and life. They are there for a reason, and we can, and should, use them as a guide rather than a barrier. Blocking your feelings will not do you any service—on the contrary, you will spend valuable time and energy trying *not to* feel them. Trying to avoid your feelings leads to impediment and this is, after all, the opposite of what you're after.

Feelings are your guide. Trust them, let yourself experience them, and release the emotional block to achieve success.

> To learn more about the EBIQ Method course click here
> www.theebiq.com

Perception

Perception is the ability to see, hear, or become aware of something through the senses. Our senses interpret reality for us. The way I see it, reality is almost always in your favor, and it is neither good nor bad, unless in an extreme situation such as war, abuse etc. Although it is mostly favorable, we interpret it based on our early experiences. Those experiences created our thoughts, and those thoughts generate feelings that stop us from showing up and playing big.

Remember those glasses I mentioned earlier? They are your thoughts and beliefs and they can distort your vision. Our thoughts are created based on our impression, which is part of how we perceive the world through our early experiences. Those thoughts create feelings, and if we change the thought we will change the feeling. That's why I say that feelings are thoughts in motion. Our thoughts and feelings are tangled in a way that is hard to separate unless you release the emotions to achieve a clearer vision, and this is where the EBIQ Method comes in. Thoughts and beliefs are the glasses through which we perceive the world, and they also distort our vision.

Two people who watch the same play or read the same book will get different things out of it and pay attention to details the other didn't even notice. This is what happens to us in real life situations, too. Reality is merely a perception of the person who interprets it.

The reason two people can look at the same situation and see something totally different is perception—it's not about what our sensors receive; it's about how our brain understands the message, and this goes back to our experiences and the beliefs they created.

I want to take you back, for a moment, to the previous chapters where I discussed the power of emotional release and how to use it to get a clearer vision of reality. The beliefs are a fog or mist on the lenses of your glasses, and by releasing emotions you're sweeping a cloth across the lenses and cleaning them. The EBIQ Method is your cloth.

My Experience with Perception:

For many years I was captivated by the notion that I didn't have what it takes to build a business. That, as someone who grew up in a small community in a foreign country, I didn't know how to connect with locals and they had no interest in hearing what I had to say. Oh boy, my perceptions were so wrong. They were old feelings of not being seen and not being encouraged to achieve excellence that shaped this point of view.

When I started my cooking business, it was hard for me to accept that I bring something fresh to the table and that people want to learn from me. I felt small, insignificant, and as if people looked down to me. It was all in my head, and luckily I realized it in time. That's why I used the EBIQ Method right from the beginning. I had to find a way to gain new perspective. I knew the old glasses shaped by my thoughts and early experiences were distorting my perception, and that would stop me from growing my business if I didn't pay attention to it.

Working on those feelings in a listening partnership

allowed me to release the emotional block, repair my glasses, and grow my business.

Affirmations

I find affirmations to be one of the best ways to repair distortions. Everything you think or say to yourself, whether it is good or bad, is an affirmation. If you reprimand yourself on a daily basis, this affirms that you're not good enough, while if you praise yourself you affirm your own goodness. That's why affirmations are a great contradiction to your setback patterns—you can create an affirmation that will state the opposite of what your setback pattern tells you, to encourage emotional release.

I want you to understand that every belief you have about yourself is just a thought, and a thought can be changed. Insecurities, moments of self-doubt, or fears are just thoughts and they can be replaced with positive thoughts of certainty, faith, and trust.

Use the EBIQ Method to identify the setback patterns and contradict them with an affirmation.

My Experience with Affirmations:
Immigrating to a new country is hard beyond words. Suddenly,

you're thrown into a game, and you're not familiar with its rules. Not only is the language one you've never used to express more than a few words, but the cultural differences are overwhelming—things that used to be unacceptable are every day now.

Your whole being is crushed, and you need to reinvent yourself and change your behavior to fit the new game. This is not only hard, but brings up old insecurities and questions about the essence of your being. You pay more attention to what needs to be improved, rather than what works.

When I moved to the US, although it was a longtime dream of mine and I was 100% sure this was the right path for me, I faced the harsh reality of isolation and lack of social support. Not having someone to call when I was down put me in a very difficult place—I felt I was losing my identity, as well as my confidence. The thoughts I had were, "No one will hire you," "You have no chance competing with the locals for a job," and, "You will never be as good as a native speaker."

Those thoughts were discouraging and didn't serve me.

In order to raise myself up I needed to embrace my feelings, so I allowed myself to cry when the kids were at the daycare. I would drop them off and go back home to lie in my bed and let the feelings flood me, without trying to control them. After letting everything out, I was able to phrase the affirmations that would help me carry myself out of the situation and get back on track.

Some of the affirmations I came up with were:

"I'm a dream come true for any employer."

"I'm mastering the new language."

"I'm smart and talented, and I can achieve anything."

I wrote those sentences on a piece of paper and affirmed myself at least three times a day, that I was capable, smart, and things would work out for me. Not long after, I found my first job in the US as a chocolatier in a small chocolate shop in town.

Affirmations in Action

Affirmations are also great contradictions to your setback patterns, since they show you what you feel is different to reality. The reality is always that you're capable and can achieve anything you focus on, while the setback pattern tells a different story to keep you safe.

Use affirmations as a gateway to your feelings, so you can release the emotional charge that keeps you from playing big.

Here's an example of how I used an affirmation to activate the release process:

Me: *I feel stuck. I need to find more clients but there's so much competition. The other people in my industry are so articulate and sophisticated. I will never get to their level...*

My Listening Partner: *Do you remember the affirmation you came up with last week to contradict that feeling?*

(My listening partner knows me, my setback patterns, and what helps me release, and that's why she suggested that direction.)

Me: *No, can you remind me?*

(This is where my setback pattern made me forget how powerful I am—I totally forgot about this affirmation.)

My Listening Partner: *"I'm smart and talented, and I can achieve anything." Can you repeat that?*

Me: *This is nonsense. Did I come up with that?*

(This is where my setback pattern argued with my growth potential.)

My Listening Partner: *Yes, you did, because you're smart and you know how powerful you are. Just repeat after me: "I'm smart and talented, and I can achieve anything."*

(This is where she insisted I should say the affirmation out loud.)

Me: *"I'm smart and talented, and I can achieve anything."*

My Listening Partner*: Say it one more time.*

Me*: "I'm smart and talented, and I can achieve anything."*

(This is where a tear came out, which means this is a good contradiction to my setback pattern. From this moment on, my partner's job was to keep the flow and allow me to release the emotions.)

My Listening Partner: *You're right, you are smart and talented, and you can achieve anything.*

(Pay attention to the fact she changed the sentence from "I am" to "you are"—this is because hearing someone else affirming that we're good and capable is a huge contradiction and can expedite the release process.)

Me: **Crying**

(At that point, when I was already releasing, all I needed to do was connect with the feeling that I'm capable, and that any other thought is simply a setback pattern.)

> The release process happens naturally when you can tell your setback pattern is different than reality.

Courage

Growing a business takes courage, determination, and self-awareness. It's all about putting yourself out there, showing the world who you are, and speaking your truth, which can be uncomfortable. These are not easy things to do because they activate fears, self-doubt, and discouragement.

The origin of the word "courage" is from the Latin word "*cor,*" which means heart. In one of its earliest forms, according to one of my favorite authors, Brené Brown, the word courage meant "To speak one's mind by telling all one's heart." This means it takes courage to be who we are and speak our truth because it puts us in a vulnerable place. Having your own business means you're not only putting yourself out there, but you're speaking your truth, which is what courage is all about.

In order to release emotions, I suggest you practice saying, in a session, what you're afraid of saying outside of a listening partnership. Practice saying the things you're too afraid to say to your friends/family/clients, and let your emotions do the work. The more releasing you do, the easier it will become to share your core with others.

For me, it meant talking about the EBIQ Method and how, by showing big emotions, you will help grow your business and take your professional life to the next level. It took a lot of courage on my end to speak my truth because I was afraid I'd be labeled as a crazy person. I had to take my feeling into a listening partnership so I'd be able to teach this to others. I was so terrified of what people would think of me, that they would no longer take me seriously, that I was paralyzed by fear and was not able to step up and show the world who I really am.

From my experience when practicing courage, fear comes up a lot—how obvious, right? This where shaking can be very beneficial. You can say all the things that make you want crawl out of your own skin and hide and tremble while saying them. Shaking is the best way to get rid of fears. Look at young children who let their bodies shake when they are terrified. They don't need to learn how to do it; it comes naturally to them.

That's the beauty of the EBIQ. We use a natural healing mechanism to help us grow and play big in our business and life.

Uncomfortable Conversations

Tim Ferris said in his book *The 4-Hour Workweek* that a person's success in life can usually be measured by the number of uncomfortable conversations he or she is willing to have, and I agree. In the growth process, you'll have many uncomfortable conversations with your partner, friends, business partner, bank, etc. These conversations should be planned as much as possible, and I recommend you have them when your mind is clear and sharp. To do that, you'll need to release emotional charge prior to the conversation, and that can be done within your listening partnership.

An Example

Lucy has a small acupuncture business she operates while raising her four kids. You can only imagine how much support she needs to take that on, especially from her partner. Lucy wrote her book with me, and when she got stuck, we identified she felt her partner didn't support her writing the book—he felt she spent too much time on her business and too little with her family. In order to get her unstuck, I simply listened to her and encouraged her to express rage. She was pissed that he wasn't supportive, and we needed to let it out in order to finish the book.

I held a pillow while Lucy hit it and yelled at me, as if I were her partner, all the things she hadn't told him. After doing it, the anger turned into sadness and she started crying.

Releasing anger and sadness helped her get unstuck, and she was able to go back to writing, and to have an open and loving conversation with her partner about her needs.

Lucy is not the only one who experienced lack of

support. Many women go through that phase when growing their business. I, personally, spent many hours releasing on this same topic, as well as other topics that allowed me to have many uncomfortable conversations.

Decide, Act, Release

Everything you do in your life and business starts with a decision. To grow your business you need to decide and then act on your decision. You need to come up with a plan and execute it. Nothing will change in your life and business if you do not execute your goals, if you keep them as "wannabes" or wishes—the secret is to take action, to execute, to move forward. Although taking action is what makes magic happen, it is also scary as hell. Taking action is about taking a risk and this can be terrifying, especially for women because we aren't encouraged to take risks.

The EBIQ Method is all about helping you take the actions that will help you grow your business, and there's a simple system to that:

1. **Make a Decision**—Let's say to hire a coach.
2. **Act On It**—Make a payment.

3. **Release**—Whatever emotion comes up, take it to a listening partnership and release it.

In the past I would suggest my clients decide, release, and then act, but then I noticed that some of them took weeks or months to just release the emotions, and they never acted on their decisions. This didn't make sense to me because only actions bring results. I realized that they should take actions first, and then use the EBIQ Method to process their feelings and to release the setback patterns. The more you release, the easier it becomes to take another action.

Chapter Summary

1. Thoughts create reality and you can choose your thoughts to create the reality you want. Use the EBIQ Method to release old beliefs.
2. Perception is a fog or mist on the lenses of your glasses, and by releasing emotions you're sweeping a cloth across the lenses and cleaning them.
3. Use an affirmation to activate the emotional release process.
4. Growing a business takes courage because it's about speaking your truth, which is scary.
5. "A person's success in life can usually be measured by the number of uncomfortable conversations he or she is willing to have" (Tim Ferris). The EBIQ Method will allow you to release emotional charge prior to an uncomfortable conversation, so you can be focused and present.
6. Use the EBIQ Method to release emotions that come up when you act on your decisions and goals.

Action Items

- Write a list of ten affirmations and read them every day for 30 days, before you go to bed and first thing in the morning. Print 3 copies and keep one in your wallet, one next to your bed, and one on your desk.

Ally Nathaniel

Chapter 10: Daily Practices

Although simple and intuitive, the EBIQ Method requires practice and commitment. Because it necessitates the open expression of emotions, practicing might feel a bit out of your comfort zone and uncomfortable at the beginning.

Trust me, the more you practice, the more natural it will feel and the easier expressing emotions will be. Think of the EBIQ Method as a muscle that was neglected for many years—it is out of shape and needs some serious stretching and massaging. Unless you take care of that muscle and give it what it needs, you will never get it back in shape. Getting this muscle back into shape will allow you to run faster and a greater distance, which means growing your business, influencing more lives, and making more money. Isn't that what you're after?

It is important you find a way to make the EBIQ Method a part of your weekly or even daily routine. Ideally, I would like you to have a one-on-one weekly session with your listening partner and join a group for a biweekly class. The class's purpose is to break the isolation, remind you that you're not alone, and keep you on top of the EBIQ Method practice and theory. The class is where you'll get group support and where you'll find people who think fondly of you and your business. This is where you'll get the encouragement and support you need in order to move forward, try new things, take risks, and grow your business.

Groups also have a type of energy that can't be found anywhere else—this is where people get together to support each other with achieving a common goal. In our case it is a group of people who speaks the same language (the EBIQ Method language), and get together to help each other grow their businesses through emotional release.

In this chapter, I will show you how to make the EBIQ Method a natural part of your daily routine, so once you implement and practice it you will not understand how you lived without it. It will be as if you grew a new arm or leg that you didn't know was missing, but now you can't see yourself living without it.

As mentioned earlier, making the decision to make the EBIQ Method a part of your life and practice daily is what will get you from where you are now to where you want to be. Knowing the theory is not enough—practicing is what will create a motion of feelings and actions that will then help you make decisions, act on them, and take your business to the next level.

Listening Partnership Sessions

This is the core partnership of the EBIQ. You can have your sessions with anyone in the world using video platforms, or with someone you meet face-to-face. From my experience, having a listening partner you meet with in person is much more powerful, especially because it provides a contradiction to our isolation patterns. Isolation is a setback pattern most of us have, and it is rooted in our past.

An Example

When Sarah was very young—four or five years old, every time she felt lonely, insecure, or sad she would cry. She craved connections, but her parents worked late and she spent many hours by herself. No wonder when they finally came home, and during the weekends, she would start crying or misbehaving without a visible cause. All she wanted was a connection with her parents, and she figured out letting her emotions out would help her feel more grounded and connected. Of course, she couldn't explain that to herself because she was very young, but her body and soul knew this was exactly what she needed to do—so she cried and threw tantrums so she could get rid of all the emotional charge that prevented her from feeling connected.

Her parents, who had no idea about the importance of

emotional release, like most parents don't, used to send her to her room until "she came to her senses." You see, she craved connection, and they isolated her. They didn't do it on purpose—they were taught this was the right way to deal with "misbehavior," and they were doing what their parents did to them. Sarah was just using her natural healing mechanism of emotional release. She didn't need to learn about it; it was implemented in her since the day she was born, and she was punished for it.

What Sarah learned was that:

1. Showing emotions is dangerous—you'll be punished for it.
2. Whenever you feel bad and show it, you are isolated.

Isolation was the opposite of what she needed, and it created a pattern in her. As she grew up she learned it was better to isolate herself whenever she was sad, angry, or upset before someone else would "send her to her room." You see, she was protecting herself from being humiliated by isolating herself, and this became her setback pattern.

Many of us, like Sarah, learned at a very young age that showing emotions and trying to heal ourselves through a natural process is socially unacceptable. There's no wonder we keep everything in and try to look strong on the outside. The problem is that it doesn't work, and the more we do it the harder it gets to heal and play big. This is why re-learning how to use your emotions to grow, and being part of an EBIQ Method group, is crucial to your success. This will break the isolation and provide the support you need to grow your business.

Participating in listening partnership sessions and being part of a group will allow you to break the isolation and practice the tool. Remember, you have to commit and show up!

Commitment

Unless you make the decision to trust and commit to the EBIQ Method it will not work for you. This is, by the way, true in all walks of life—without commitment nothing is possible. Commitment means that you choose to place your focus on what you know will help you advance your business or life and you don't back down.

Commitment means that, no matter what happens, you get out of bed and do the work. No matter what happens, you stick with your plan and trust the process. Commitment means that you make it a priority to meet with your listening partner and your group on a weekly basis, and, no matter what happens—your dog got a cold, your aunt is visiting, or there's a new hit TV show you want to binge watch—you are not negotiating about the EBIQ Method and its necessity. You get out of bed, get out of the house, and get to work on your setback patterns. As it is, or as much as you don't feel like it, you meet with your listening partner to do the work. You meet with them because, unless you release the emotional blocks that are attached to your setback patterns, it will be almost impossible to grow your business. You'll get stuck and sabotage your growth over and over again.

What to Release On?

As you grow your business you will need to release your emotional blocks around topics that are crucial to business growth. Those topics are at the core of your setback patterns, and paying attention to them will help you move forward faster. Choosing specific topics to concentrate on in your listening partnership sessions is a smart idea. That way you are not only leading the way, but also taking control over your own growth.

The most tremendous growth I've experienced, both for myself and my clients, happened when I chose to concentrate on a specific topic for a significant period of time. That means I made a decision and committed to looking into my setback patterns around money, for example, for at least three sessions (preferably more). This allowed me to dig deep into the patterns and beliefs that feel so familiar to me, and therefore safe. Choosing a specific topic to work on also allowed my listening partner to hold me accountable for my goals.

You see, your listening partner is there not only to listen to you and help you release emotional tangles and setback patterns, but also to hold you accountable. They will not only remind you what your goals are, but will encourage you to dig deeper into your own beliefs when you don't feel like doing it.

Looking inside, digging deep, and going back to our early experiences is not always pleasant. Actually, most times it's the opposite—it's rough and painful and annoying and boring, and it makes you feel like you want to run away and hide. Your instinct is to avoid re-experiencing that time of your life at all costs. You buried it as deep as possible and covered it with a thick layer of dirt. It makes you feel that way because the original experience was painful and most likely you had no support back then. This is why people will spend years trying to make detours instead of dealing with what causes they're present struggles—it is simply too hard.

I assume that whatever experience you had as a child, you tried as hard as you could to heal yourself from it—you might have cried, or yelled, or tried to hit someone, or had a big tantrum. You did everything in your power to feel safe and connected and loved again, but the adults around you didn't get it. They sent you to your room, isolating you. They told you that you were grounded for a week because you misbehaved or they even punished you physically—they slapped you or maybe hit you with a belt.

There are many methods to keep kids in their place and to scare them so they'll behave. Not only the experience itself was hurtful (the kids in the classroom made fun of you, your older brother took your favorite toy, or you were not allowed to play with someone you liked), but the reaction from the adults around you made it even worse.

You were smart, so you learned to hide any big emotional reactions, to isolate yourself before someone else did, not to ask for help because it was not available, and to pretend things are OK when they are a complete mess. That "smart" behavior turned into a pattern. You practiced it for a long time, and it saved you from getting hurt over and over again. Don't get me wrong, I truly believe it was smart of you to do that back then—it saved you a lot of shame and embarrassment, and it was right to choose that path when nothing else was available to you.

Although it was the right solution back then, as you grew

older and built your business those behavioral patterns got in your way. Isolating yourself when things get rough, or pretending as if everything is OK when things are turning sour, turns into an obstacle. Those patterns (and you might have other patterns than those I've described) are basically holding you back from growing.

This is why I recommend releasing on those topics, because they are crucial not only for business growth, but for improving your life.

Bring those topics into your listening partnership and release on each one of them. It is up to you to choose which one to work on first and which one to keep for last, but I highly recommend releasing on all of them because each topic/area might be holding you back in your business in some way.

In the following section, I'll be suggesting topics to work on and release the emotional tangles attached to them. Take every suggestion from the list below and examine it in your listening session. Pay close attention to the feelings that come up, and do your best to release the emotions that are tangled with your thoughts and experiences. If a statement makes you laugh or cry, go for it. Keep releasing the emotion until you're done.

Your listening partner can repeat a statement or idea as long as it helps you release. Keep in mind that we tend to stop ourselves from releasing. It might be in a form of self-talk—that little voice in your head that warns you from crying too hard or laughing too loud. Remind yourself that you're in a safe place and the whole purpose is to release emotional tangles. Cry hard, laugh loud, hit pillows, yell, or even brag about how great you are—be as loud and clear as possible. Doing that will help you get over your fears and try new things, which in turn will help you grow your business.

It's all about emotional cleansing—a healthy soul will produce better results.

Below are suggestions for topics I recommend concentrating on. These topics are usually heavily tied up with mental blocks and setback patterns that are preventing you from taking actions to grow your businesses. You can start by choosing the topic that feels like it is the core of your inability to take actions or to make changes that will allow your business to grow. Trust your mind to lead you to what you need to work on. Ultimately, I want you to release on all the topics, but first commit to work on one for three sessions or more.

Money

What did your parents teach you about money?
- Is money the root of all evil?
- Does money grow on trees?
- Do you have to sweat to make money?
- Are you allowed to talk about money?
- Are there any people in your family who have made it? Who are they and what you think of them?
- What did your parents teach you about money?
- What is your first memory related to money?
- Is money good, evil?
- What's the first thought that comes to mind when you hear the word "money?"
- Rich people are….
- Poor people are…
- Is making money hard/easy?
- What would happen if you were rich?
- How much money did your dad/mom make at your age? If you make more how does it make you feel? If you make less, how does it feel?
- What does having no money feel like?
- Did it ever happen that you had no money at all? What

was it like?
- Do you sometimes feel as if you don't have enough money? Is it reality or a fear?

Start by asking yourself those questions and pay close attention to the emotions they bring up. This is a great opportunity to investigate your beliefs and setback patterns. It's also a great opportunity to look into your family beliefs and what you inherited from your parents, grandparents, and their grandparents. Once you're able to recognize that a belief is an inheritance, and not necessarily yours, you have the power to choose whether you want to accept it or not. This is super powerful when creating the life you want for yourself. The fact that your dad thought money doesn't grow on trees doesn't mean you can't be good at making money. You see, it is always about tracking the origins and making a conscious choice.

Although inherited setback patterns feel very real and as if they're part of who you are, don't be mistaken. Differentiating your beliefs from your inheritance is a powerful tool—if it's not yours, you don't have to keep it, and you don't have to believe in it anymore. You can release it and make room for positive beliefs and growth.

Money is a heavy topic in the sense that there are many secrets hiding around it (similar to sex). People tend to give it meanings that are beyond the simple truth that money is a form of energy and it is neither evil nor good—it is benign.

Once you feel the need to laugh, cry, yell, or any other form of emotional release, let it all out.

Your First Memory Connected to Money

A "flash-answer" is a great technique to access your earliest memories. A flash answer is when someone asks you a question and your answer is the first thing that comes to mind. No need to think it through; just trust your mind to take you to the right place, even if sometimes it makes no sense. Once you answer, keep talking about this memory, dig deep, and explore the feelings connected to it. Let your mind wander and connect the dots, and once an emotion comes up, release it.

The best way to use this technique is to ask your listening partner to ask you, **"What's your first memory connected to money?"** Then follow that question as described above. As you work through your money beliefs, you'll notice a change in your business: in your ability to ask for money, to raise prices, to offer your programs, and more.

Asking For Help

What does asking for help mean to you?
- Was help available to you as a young child?
- Did you get any help when you asked for it?
- Were you allowed to ask for help?
- Were you humiliated/ridiculed when asked for help?
- What's your earliest memory of asking for help?
- What does asking for help look like in your family?
- Is asking for help a weakness or strength?
- People who ask for help are…
- When was the last time you asked for help, and what was the outcome?
- I shouldn't ask for help because…

For many people, things gets very hard when they need help, when they can't do everything by themselves anymore, and when they need to figure out something new. At a certain age asking for help is considered a weakness (especially in men), and we're encouraged to keep it to ourselves and to try figure out the solution before we address an adult. Yes, figuring out things by yourself is a useful life skill, but society's reactions push us to keep trying even when we fail over and over again without reaching out for help. If asking for help is a weakness, who wants to be weak? We keep doing that in our businesses—trying over and over again, instead of hiring someone who can teach us what we need to know.

Contradictive affirmations you can use:
- Help is available to me whenever I need it.
- People are thrilled to help or assist me.
- Asking for help makes me stronger.

What's Your Earliest Memory of Asking For Help?

Use flash-answers to find this memory. As mentioned earlier, your listening partner can ask you **"What's your earlier memory of asking for help?"** Your job is to say the first thing that comes up, even if it doesn't make sense in the moment. This answer provides a gateway to deeper thoughts and beliefs, which might lead to the core of your setback pattern. Trust your mind that it will take you to the right place, and that whatever comes up is exactly what you need to work on. Your purpose is to release the emotional charge tangled with this experience.

Making Decisions (I don't know)

- Is making decisions natural to you?
- What was the first decision you made in your life?
- How were you treated when you voiced your decision?
- Who made the decisions at home?
- Are men better at making decisions than women?
- It's better not to decide because…
- If I don't make a decision I'm…
- People who make quick decisions are…
- Hesitating means that…

Making a decision is not an easy task. Making decisions is about saying "yes" to one opportunity while losing another. It's about knowing what you want and going for it. No wonder this is so hard for so many business owners—if you choose X you might lose Y, if you say "no" to an opportunity, who knows if you'll ever get it back?

Men are trained to be decisive and make decisions more than women are. That's the reason girls and women are more likely to answer with "I don't know." Actually, for many years I used to answer that way. It was not because I didn't know what I wanted, but because I knew no one cared. More than that, if you want something big, if your dreams are wild, they will immediately be shot down if you voice them, and if you can't voice your dreams, you can't make a decision. It is as simple as that.

Practice Making Decisions

- I'm going to write a letter to…
- I'm going to tell my husband how I feel.
- I'm going to hire a coach.
- I'm going to take out a loan.

The listening partnership environment is a perfect place to practice decision-making and notice what comes up for you. You can simply state, "I will get a loan for $20,000 tomorrow," and notice what feelings arise. Fear is highly likely to show up for you when making a decision, and this is a great opportunity to notice that and release the emotional charge.

Bragging

The definition of bragging is "to say in a boastful manner," and has a negative connotation. But what if you simply state something true about yourself? Is that bragging? What if you say, "I'm good at math," or, "I'm a talented writer,"—is that bragging? I think not.

The problem is whenever someone states a positive affirmation about themselves they're immediately dismissed as boastful. No one wants to be that way, so we stop encouraging ourselves with positive affirmations.

When it comes to business, you have to be clear about the things you're good at, and what's a better way than stating them out loud? That's why I suggest bringing bragging into your listening partnership session, where you can investigate your feelings around who you really are, your strengths, and the messages you got when you were proud of being good at something.

In the session, use a boastful tone—it will help you get rid of the fear, shame, and other feelings tied up with bragging. When you're done, you'll be able to notice the difference between your talent and achievement and your emotions.

- I'm the best writer in town.
- I'm the most talented chess player.
- What can I say? Business is my talent.

Keep releasing on those topics and others, until you get rid of enough setback patterns and are able to think rationally and act on your business growth.

Chapter Summary

1. Joining an EBIQ Method group and committing to the process is crucial to keep you on track. It provides structure and support.
2. Release emotions on specific topics that are holding you back, such as money, asking for help, making decisions, and more.
3. Bragging is a great way to notice what you're good at and what emotions are tangled to stating the talent or achievement.

Chapter 11: Now Is What Counts

Now that you're almost done reading this book, you're probably asking yourself, "What's next?" What do I need to do in order to take on the EBIQ Method and use it to grow my business? What do I need to do to make this practice part of my life? Those are great questions!

The answer you're looking for is: Start practicing now. Find a listening partner and start now. Join an EBIQ Method group and make this method part of your life. You get it, the main idea is to not waste any more time, to start practicing. The thing is that decisive people are action takers, and that's why they're the ones who are most successful both in business and life. Make a decision to add the EBIQ Method to your life and act on your decision.

Done is the New Perfect

That's what I always tell my clients. Getting something done is ten times better than getting it perfect. It is better to write a book and get it published today than to perfect it for 20 years until you lose momentum and never get it published.

There's power in acting now. There's power in executing. It shows the universe that you are serious about being successful, and, therefore, it will support you. The "Law of Action" is a universal law that states action must be taken in order for us to manifest things on earth. To support our thoughts, dreams, emotions, and words, we must engage in action first. It's about performing the actions necessary to achieve what you are setting out to do. Unless you take actions toward what you want to accomplish, there will be absolutely no foreseeable results.

Since many people fail on that premise, because they never take action, I want you to be aware and avoid that pitfall. This is why most people falter when pursuing success. Don't be like them—take action and join an EBIQ Method group today. Find a listening partner, find a support group, and start releasing the emotions that are stopping you from taking action and growing your business and life.

Where to Start

To learn more about the EBIQ Method or how to connect with

me, join a group, or become a group facilitator, go to the EBIQ Method website and send me a message.

Practicing the EBIQ Method takes some learning first. Although you have the basis for the method from this book, you will not be able to use it correctly until you practice. That's why I want you to contact me today for more information about groups in your area or online.

Stop Wasting Time

Remember, growing your business is totally doable. Many people have done exactly that before you and I were even born, and many will do it after we are long gone. Although people have been able to achieve massive success with very little resource or support, for many others the day-to-day struggle as well as the emotional rollercoaster becomes too much to bear, and therefore they quit. They quit because of isolation and because of lack of support and guidance. They quit because they don't have the emotional tools to deal with what growing a business takes.

Many people also quit because what they've been told about how to manage and grow a business does not align with reality. They've been told to suck it up and move on. They've been told to act tough and never show emotion, and that's not how they operate in this world, especially not women. The gap between what is "right" when growing a business and what is "wrong" is simply too confusing for many and they get lost.

There is another way, a better way. A way where you can not only show emotions, but use them to grow our business and flourish. This way is called the Emotional Business IQ Method, and it was created to serve you and others like yourself, who understand the importance of emotions and connection for growth.

So stop wasting time. Sign up for the EBIQ Method program and start growing your business while eliminating time wastage and emotional hurdles. Get out there today and use the method to seize your moment.

You matter, your mission matters, and your business matters, and I'm here to support you.

> Click here to learn more about the EBIQ Method and community
> http://www.theebiq.com

Glossary of EBIQ Method Terms

Intentional Listening – Where a person listens to another person with full attention, thinking about their well-being and how to help them release emotions.

Client – The person who's being listened to.

Rational Thinking – The state we aspire to be in at all times, where we can make decisions based on data rather than our emotions.

Listening Partnership – The basic EBIQ Method setup where two or more people are listening to each other, intentionally.

Session – The time where two or more people are engaged in a listening partnership.

Emotional release – Where the "client" releases emotions using their natural healing mechanism.

Statement – A phrase or a sentence used during the session to help the "client" notice their setback pattern is different than reality.

Contradiction – A statement suggested in a listening partnership by the listener, to point out a client's setback pattern and promote emotional release.

Patterns – The behavioral or mental patterns

installed in us by our families and society, which are holding us back from achieving greatness in business and life.

Re-activation – When our patterns are activated by a present incident or situation and block us from thinking and acting rationally.

Early Hurt – The source of all patterns. Created by recurring mistreatment, usually in early childhood.

EMOTIONAL RELEASE CHART

Emotion	Manifestation During Release
Grief	Tears, Sobbing
Heavy fears	Trembling, shivering, cold perspiration, need to urinate
Light fears such as embarrassment	Laughter, cold perspiration
Heavy angers	Angry noises, violent movements, warm perspiration
Light angers	Laughter, warm perspiration
Boredom	Laughter, animated talking, reluctant talking
Physical pain and tension	Yawns, stretching, scratching

- This chart is based on the "discharge indications and sequence chart" from the fundamentals of co-counseling manual.

www.ingramcontent.com/pod-product-compliance
Lightning Source LLC
Chambersburg PA
CBHW070642220526
45466CB00001B/264